THE SINGAPORE SYNTHESIS

INNOVATION · INCLUSION · INSPIRATION

IPS-NATHAN LECTURES

THE SINGAPORE SYNTHESIS

INNOVATION · INCLUSION · INSPIRATION

RAVI MENON

Published by

World Scientific Publishing Co. Pte. Ltd.
5 Toh Tuck Link, Singapore 596224
USA office: 27 Warren Street, Suite 401-402, Hackensack, NJ 07601
UK office: 57 Shelton Street, Covent Garden, London WC2H 9HE

National Library Board, Singapore Cataloguing in Publication Data
Name(s): Menon, Ravi.
Title: The Singapore synthesis : innovation, inclusion, inspiration / Ravi Menon.
Other Title(s): IPS-Nathan Lecture series ; 9
Description: Singapore : World Scientific Publishing Co. Pte. Ltd., [2022]
Identifier(s): ISBN 978-981-12-5107-8 (hardcover) | ISBN 978-981-12-5145-0 (paperback) |
    ISBN 978-981-12-5108-5 (ebook for institutions) |
    ISBN 978-981-12-5109-2 (ebook for individuals)
Subject(s): LCSH: Singapore--Economic policy. | Singapore--Social policy. |
    Technological innovations--Singapore. | Equality--Singapore. |
    National characteristics, Singaporean.
Classification: DDC 959.57--dc23

British Library Cataloguing-in-Publication Data
A catalogue record for this book is available from the British Library.

For any available supplementary material, please visit
https://www.worldscientific.com/worldscibooks/10.1142/12690#t=suppl

Desk Editor: Lai Ann

Typeset by Stallion Press
Email: enquiries@stallionpress.com

THE S R NATHAN FELLOWSHIP FOR THE STUDY OF SINGAPORE

AND THE IPS-NATHAN LECTURE SERIES

The S R Nathan Fellowship for the Study of Singapore was established by the Institute of Policy Studies (IPS) in 2013 to support research on public policy and governance issues. With the generous contributions of individual and corporate donors, and a matching government grant, IPS raised around S$5.9 million to endow the Fellowship.

Each S R Nathan Fellow, appointed under the Fellowship, delivers a series of IPS-Nathan Lectures during his or her term. These public lectures aim to promote public understanding and discourse on issues of critical national interest.

The Fellowship is named after Singapore's sixth and longest-serving President, the late S R Nathan, in recognition of his lifetime of service to Singapore.

IPS-Nathan Lectures

Print ISSN: 2630-4996
Online ISSN: 2630-5003

CONTENTS

FOREWORD

Mr Ravi Menon speaking at the first lecture of his IPS-Nathan Lecture series
Source: Jacky Ho for the Institute of Policy Studies

This series of lectures springs out of a conviction that Singapore can do better.

Singapore's remarkable development since independence in 1965 is a story of boldness in vision and tenacity in execution. It owes in large part to what I have termed the "Singapore Synthesis" — an imaginative and judicious blend of diverse ideologies and approaches, drawing from policies and practices from around the world. An ethos of adaptation, meritocracy and pragmatism permeated the *Singapore Synthesis*.

It is also my conviction that the best chapters of the Singapore Story have yet to be written, and that to write them we need a refreshed *Singapore Synthesis* — a more innovative economy, a more inclusive society, and a more inspiring nation. As a country, we are moving in the right direction on all three fronts, but too tentatively, too incrementally. In Singapore, it has become more respectable to err on the side of caution than on the side of boldness.

These lectures make the case for a higher level of ambition, a faster pace of change, and a greater willingness to take risks.

The first lecture sets the stage, describing four driving forces that will transform economies and societies globally: ageing demographics, rising inequality, technological disruption, and climate change. These tectonic shifts, coupled with an increasingly ambiguous geopolitical landscape and the spectre of an age of pandemics, not to mention a delicate domestic political transition, portend an operating environment that is highly uncertain and complex.

But uncertainty cannot be a reason for gradualism, and complexity should not obscure clarity of purpose. Our journey cannot be one of merely solving the problems that come our way; it must be guided by a vision of what we want to be and how we want to get there. At the same time, we must see the world for what it is and not what we wish it to be. The *Singapore Synthesis* is about holding idealism and realism in equal measure.

The second lecture spells out why innovation must be at the heart of the new economy. It highlights three areas where innovation can potentially deliver substantial economic gains: making our domestic services exportable; transforming our economy to be digital end-to-end; and taking the lead in Asia as the vanguard of a green economy. As with all innovation, these moves are not without risk, especially of rising costs and some job displacement. But not making these moves leaves Singapore at even greater risk: of an unequal, dual economy; a digitally fragmented ecosystem; and getting stranded in a net zero world.

The third lecture presents a job-centred model of social inclusion. It aims to lift low-wage workers, sustain median wage growth, temper wealth inequality and promote income mobility. This model of inclusion comprises safety nets in the form of a minimum wage and an enhanced workfare income supplement, for a basic level of support; a trampoline in the form of re-employment support to help people bounce back if they fall; and four escalators to help people move up along a trajectory of rising wages — namely, an expanded progressive wage model, reclaiming mid-level jobs for Singaporeans, professionalising all jobs, and life-long learning.

The fourth lecture paints a vision of an inspiring nation, driven by purpose and based on values. There is a risk to bear in becoming a more innovative economy and a price to pay in creating a more inclusive society. The choices we make will boil down to values: who we are, and what we stand for. I have shared my thoughts on five values-based attributes that could make Singapore an inspiring nation: a meritocracy of hope that is broad, inclusive, and compassionate; a beacon for diversity that is open to the world and alternative views; a city of giving driven by a spirit of volunteerism and philanthropy; a heart for the environment prompting us to do the right thing for a sustainable future; and a thousand points of light shining from an active citizenry, an innovative business community, an energetic civil society, a vibrant academia, and many other sources of strength brightening and energising our nation.

There is coherence across the ideas in the *Singapore Synthesis*. Making our domestic services more productive and exportable goes hand in hand with digitalising business processes end-to-end, professionalising all jobs, and fostering a broad and inclusive meritocracy. The transition to a high-productivity, high-wage, high-cost economy will not be without dislocations, which is why strengthened safety nets and trampolines to support workers are critical. The impetus for restructuring towards a greener economy comes not only from economic incentive but a societal value, with people having a heart for the environment and willing to pay a price today for a more sustainable world tomorrow. The social consensus in favour of global talent, open markets, and wealth accumulation is stronger if there is better protection for the median Singapore worker, a more progressive taxation of wealth and a stronger spirit of philanthropy.

But ultimately, the purpose of these lectures is not to provide answers but to provoke questions. Is our paradigm of competitiveness still largely based on considerations of cost rather than value, and is that standing in the way of correctly pricing scarce resources like carbon and foreign labour? Is our model of economic and social support overly centred on protecting jobs rather than workers, on keeping firms alive rather than pushing them to restructure? Is our approach to recognition of talent still focused on qualifications rather than skills? Is our idea of professionalism still confined mainly to white-collar rather than blue-collar occupations? It is my fervent hope that these lectures help to spark fresh ideas and thoughtful conversations about the kind of economy, society, and nation we want to be.

These lectures would not have been possible without the support of many.

- Janadas Devan, Director, Institute of Policy Studies (IPS), whom I had turned down three times but whose considerable persuasive powers I eventually yielded to in taking up the S R Nathan Fellowship;
- Jacqueline Loh, for covering my duties at the Monetary Authority of Singapore on several occasions while I was immersed in preparing the lectures;
- Liang Kaixin and her dedicated team at IPS, who ensured excellent arrangements for the lectures;
- Marcus Fum, Jasmine Koh, Kwok Quek Sin, Lim Bey An, Peter Lim, Ng DingXuan, Ng Jia Jun, Damien Pang, Jacqueline Poh, Edward Robinson, Celine Sia, Tan Chorh Chuan, Tay Sulian, Thong Leng Yeng, Tu Suh Ping, and Bruno Wildermuth, for their insightful comments and suggestions;

- Abby Ang, Cyrene Chew, Li Tiansheng, Candice Low, Ng Yi Ping, Angeline Qiu, Moses Soh, Jensen Tan, and Xie Kaiwei, for their careful statistical analysis and fact checks;
- Eunice Amor Oh, my diligent research assistant from IPS who did an outstanding job putting together, often at short notice, numerous background materials and helped me in so many other ways;
- Danny Quah, Chng Kai Fong, Chua Mui Hoong, and Tan Su Shan for moderating the question-and-answer sessions following the lectures with such skill and thoughtfulness; and
- the many people from the public, private, and people sectors who wrote to me offering thanks, praise, and encouragement.

Finally, the thinking behind the *Singapore Synthesis* is the product of a lifetime of learning from friends, colleagues, mentors, and many others, here and abroad. To all of them, I owe a deep debt of gratitude.

Ravi Menon
25 October 2021

ABOUT THE MODERATORS

Danny Quah is Dean and Li Ka Shing Professor in Economics at the Lee Kuan Yew School of Public Policy, National University of Singapore. Prof Quah was previously Assistant Professor of Economics at Massachusetts Institute of Technology (MIT), and then Professor of Economics and International Development, and Director of the Saw Swee Hock Southeast Asia Centre at the London School of Economics (LSE). He served as LSE's Head of Department for Economics, and Council Member on Malaysia's National Economic Advisory Council.

Chng Kai Fong was appointed Managing Director of the Singapore Economic Development Board (EDB) on 1 October 2017. Before EDB, Mr Chng was the Principal Private Secretary to the Prime Minister. He also served in the Ministry of Trade and Industry, Civil Service College, Ministry of Home Affairs, and the Ministry of Communications and Information. As part of the Public Service's development programme, Mr Chng was seconded for two years to Shell.

Chua Mui Hoong is Associate Editor at *The Straits Times*, where she has been a journalist since 1991. She was part of the ST team that interviewed Lee Kuan Yew over several years for the book *Lee Kuan Yew: Hard Truths to Keep Singapore Going.* Her latest book *Singapore, Disrupted* (2018) is a compilation of ST essays and new writings on politics and income inequality. She was Opinion Editor at ST for nine years until 2020, and now happily works from home writing commentaries and speaking or moderating at webinars.

Tan Su Shan is Group Head of Institutional Banking at DBS, and also serves as the President Commissioner for PT Bank DBS Indonesia. Prior to leading the institutional banking business, she was Group Head of Consumer Banking and Wealth Management business for close to a decade. Before joining DBS, Ms Tan was Morgan Stanley's Head of Private Wealth Management for Southeast Asia. She has also worked at Citibank and prior to that at ING Barings in London, Tokyo and Hong Kong.

ABOUT THE COVER ILLUSTRATOR

Huang Minxian (emmecks.com) is a designer from Singapore. She graduated from the National University of Singapore in 2019, majoring in Industrial Design, and is currently working at the Institute of Policy Studies. She enjoys baking and hopes to open her own café one day.

Lecture I
THE FOUR HORSEMEN

There are some fundamental changes sweeping across the world. The *Book of Revelation* speaks of four horsemen emerging at the dawn of the Apocalypse. Interpretations of what they signify vary, but in most accounts the four horsemen symbolise *Conquest*, *War*, *Famine* and *Death*. If the horsemen represent fundamental changes to the old order, then the four horsemen today that are capable of bringing about such change are *Demographics*, *Inequality*, *Technology* and *Climate*.

Ageing demographics, rising inequality, technological disruption and climate change will together precipitate the biggest economic and societal transformation the world has seen since the Industrial Revolution. Whether they lead to Apocalypse or provide the impetus for Renaissance depends on how the global community and individual nations respond to them.

The Fifth Horseman

Given what we are going through today, is there a fifth horseman that we should consider, that is, *Pandemic*? Epidemics and pandemics have ravaged the world for centuries, with the bubonic plague in the Middle Ages estimated to have wiped out 30 to 60 per cent of Europe's population. In the last two decades, we have seen SARS, MERS and Ebola, to name a few. For 18 months now, the world has been battling the COVID-19 pandemic, which has infected more than 180 million people and taken nearly 4 million lives.

Are we on the cusp of a new Age of Pandemics? Increased interaction between humans and animals, urbanisation and overcrowding, global connectivity, and even climate change, have emerged as risk factors for what some experts believe may be new pandemics occurring more frequently, perhaps every 10 years or so.

Even if we are not looking at more frequent pandemics, COVID-19 is here to stay. Earlier this year, the UK-based scientific journal *Nature* asked more than 100 immunologists, infectious disease researchers and virologists working on COVID-19 whether the virus could be eradicated. Almost 90 per cent of the respondents said no; instead, COVID-19 will become endemic — meaning that it will continue to circulate in pockets of the global population for years to come.[1] Locking down large parts of the economy or closing borders in an effort to bring infections down to zero is futile.

In the endemic stage, COVID-19 will become less fatal or debilitating. Populations will acquire herd immunity against the virus, from mass vaccination and extensive natural infection. Several effective treatments are now available that can reduce disease severity and mortality. In the endemic phase, the number of infections roughly stabilises and societies tolerate the seasonal illnesses and deaths they bring. In fact, seasonal flu still claims roughly 650,000 lives per year globally.[2] Even in Singapore, seasonal flu is estimated to result in about 520,000 outpatient visits, 1,500 hospitalisations and 600 deaths each year.[3]

Countries that learn how to live in an endemic COVID world will do better than those who do not.

The willingness of populations to get vaccinated will be a critical success factor. Estimates vary but countries will need to vaccinate 75 to 90 per cent of their populations to reach herd immunity.[4] Herd immunity does not mean no one gets infected or no one dies of COVID-19, but by greatly reducing the risks of severe disease and death, it considerably enhances a country's ability to thrive in an endemic COVID world. Unfortunately, misinformation has led to considerable vaccine scepticism in many parts of the world.

Countries that take a risk management approach and avoid the extremes of zero tolerance or laissez-faire will do better. Countries that have chosen strategies of zero or very low tolerance for infections will have a hard time reopening their economies. Sound risk management is also key in responding judiciously to the occasional spikes in infections that will occur from time to time. Not imposing any safe management measures, especially if significant sections of the population have not been vaccinated, risks bringing on a renewed epidemic. On the other hand, closing borders and imposing lockdowns in response to every new outbreak will severely affect livelihoods with little or no gain in lives saved.

Singapore is well placed to make the transition from pandemic to endemic COVID. Singapore's strategy for now is to contain new transmissions until the population is largely vaccinated. Letting up restrictions prematurely will only prolong the pandemic situation, as many countries are tragically finding out. Moving to an endemic COVID world, we must learn to live with seasonal outbreaks with less draconian containment measures that minimise the impact on economic and social life. Testing, tracing and therapeutics will be key to achieving this: testing to pick up new infections quickly, tracing to identify and contain potential clusters, and therapeutics to treat and restore to health those who get infected. We must aim to make the recovery rate for COVID-19 close to that of seasonal flu. Then, we can live without fear.

Our aim must be to restore economic and social activities to pre-COVID levels. What will be different from pre-COVID times are likely a baseline level of safe management measures such as mask wearing and safe distancing in riskier settings or periods of heightened alert, new social norms such as not coming to work when not feeling well, and improved ventilation and fresh air exchange in our buildings. Every sizeable organisation ought to have a business continuity plan in case some form of mobility restrictions is re-imposed. This will be a key dimension of economic resilience.

In fact, pandemic resilience could be a new source of competitive advantage for Singapore. In a post-COVID future, there will be a premium on trust and stability for countries that can handle crises with minimal disruption to economic activity. Global business leaders who talk to the Economic Development Board (EDB) and the Monetary Authority of Singapore (MAS) say how Singapore's handling of the pandemic has strengthened its relative position as a resilient place to do business.

Let me now move on to the four horsemen that are likely to have an even deeper and longer-term impact on the world and pose much larger challenges to Singapore. I will be rather selective in my discussion as I try to cover all four horsemen in one lecture. My intent is to use the four horsemen to set the stage for a more focused discussion on Singapore in the next three lectures.

The First Horseman: Demographics

The first horseman — Demographics — is the most predictable of the four. His path is pre-determined and we know where he is heading.

The world is getting older. People are having fewer children and living longer. A half-century of evidence suggests that in all prosperous countries where women are well educated and free to choose whether and when to have children, fertility rates fall significantly below replacement levels.[5] Policy interventions by various countries to reverse decline in fertility have generally not succeeded.[6] The combination of declining fertility and rising life expectancy means that in the next few decades, the population of most of the world outside Africa will plateau and begin to fall — for the first time in modern history.[7]

The distribution of working-age populations across countries and regions will become highly unequal. In the next 20 years, it is projected that the proportion of the working-age in South Asia, Latin America, the Middle East and North Africa will be above 65 per cent.[8] But without adequate skills training and job creation, these countries will experience demographic burdens, not dividends.

As a corollary, various countries and regions will experience a dramatic rise in their old-age dependency ratios — the population aged 65 and above relative to the working-age population. This will be sharply felt in the developed world. In Europe and North America, it is projected to rise to 49 older persons per 100 working-age persons by 2050, up from the current 30.[9] The old-age dependency ratio is projected to more than double in East and Southeast Asia, from 18 in 2019 to 43 in 2050.[10]

Rising old-age dependency ratios could hamper economic growth. The pool of retirees will grow faster than the labour force. A greater share of national income will need to be devoted to healthcare and other social and economic support for seniors. Shifting age structures poses the risk of many developing countries in Asia becoming old before they become rich, making the middle-income trap more likely.

Fertility rates far below replacement pose particularly serious challenges. The decline in the labour force will be sharp rather than gradual and there will be a growing number of the very elderly who will require some kind of mobility assistance and personalised care.

In Singapore, the fertility rate is only about half the replacement rate. Paradoxically, the public discourse on demographics has focused on whether the population is too large or growing too fast or whether there are too many foreigners. But more significant than the size or composition of the population is the *age* of the population, in particular, the implications on an economy with a *shrinking labour force* and on a society with a *growing care gap* for the very elderly.

Shrinking Labour Force

Singapore's working-age citizen population has begun to shrink. By 2030, the proportion of citizens aged 20 to 64 is expected to decrease from 63 to 56 per cent.[11] A shrinking workforce means that productivity growth is the only source of economic growth. Increases in automation, female labour force participation and retirement age will help, but this will not be enough to offset the demographic impact on economic growth.

Immigration and intake of foreign workers are some of the more effective ways to stretch out the effects of a sharp labour force decline. It cannot be a permanent solution, because eventually, there will be physical limits to the size of population that Singapore can accommodate. But immigration can help to smoothen the transition and reduce adjustment costs on the economy and society.

The key is integration. Too rapid a rate of immigration can threaten a country's sense of identity and create anxieties of being overrun by foreigners. Countries that are able to successfully integrate immigrants into their societies have better prospects of overcoming their demographic constraints. Singapore has always been among such countries, and we must remain so. I will touch on foreign workers and immigration in all three of my next lectures.

Growing Care Gap

Singapore is one of the most rapidly ageing countries in the world. By 2030, one in four Singaporeans will be aged 65 years and above, a marked increase from the ratio of one in six in 2020 and one in 11 in 2010.[12]

There will likely be a growing gap in caregiving for the elderly. Generally, the elderly of tomorrow are likely to stay healthy much longer than those today. But while fewer are likely to have chronic or debilitating conditions, more may become prone to the ailments of the very elderly, such as dementia and Alzheimer's. Between 2000 and 2020, the number of residents aged 65 years and over who had mobility issues nearly doubled from around 25,500 to 50,000.[13]

The Second Horseman: Inequality

The second horseman — Inequality — is the most prominent and talked about horseman. He poses one of the biggest social, economic and political challenges of our time.

Dispersion in income growth is a global phenomenon. In the United States, there has been a sharp divergence in wage growth between the two ends of the income distribution. According to a recent Brookings report, between 1979 and 2018, the average real hourly wage of the bottom 20 per cent of the income distribution had more or less stagnated.[14] By contrast, the income of the top 1 per cent in the US had risen sharply by 160 per cent in the same period.[15] Along with its spectacular growth, China has also seen the world's biggest and fastest rise in inequality. A study by the China Development Research Foundation suggests that China's Gini coefficient has surged from less than 0.3 in 1978 to more than 0.48 in 2012.[16]

Technology and globalisation have been cited as the proximate drivers of the rise in income inequality. Of the two, globalisation is blamed more often, but many economists believe that skill-biased technological change is the main driver of income inequality. Technological change has dampened the demand for lower-skilled workers. By expanding opportunities for offshoring production, globalisation has had strong displacement effects in localised settings but its impact on inequality has probably not been as pervasive as that of technology.

A certain degree of income inequality is inevitable and even desirable in a market economy. Differences in rewards are necessary to spur effort and enterprise, and unequal outcomes that reflect unequal abilities are generally accepted by most people. I would suggest that inequality becomes socially unacceptable and economically inefficient when it leads to *increased poverty*, *middle-class stagnation*, a *growing wealth gap* or *reduced social mobility*. These four outcomes imply a certain permanence and erode that critical ingredient for personal endeavour, that is, hope for the future.

Increased Poverty

The central economic challenge for a very large part of the world's population is poverty, not inequality. As the late American economist Martin Feldstein puts it, the emphasis should be on eliminating poverty, and not on the overall distribution of income or the general extent of inequality.[17]

Indeed, in many developing countries, alleviating poverty is a higher priority than reducing income inequality. And rightly so. In many of these countries, economic growth has been the single most powerful factor in alleviating poverty. Growth has lifted hundreds of millions of people out of poverty in the last 50 years, in China, India, Indonesia and others.

In the developed countries, poverty is lower, more stable and not as responsive to economic growth. The US appears to be somewhat of an outlier, where the poverty rate rose significantly in the wake of the recession caused by the 2008 global financial crisis, and early research suggests that the poverty rate rose again during the COVID-19 pandemic.[18] The US poverty rate seems particularly sensitive to recessions, with some research pointing to weak social safety nets as a key factor.[19] With stronger social safety nets, European countries have had relatively more stable poverty rates through business cycles.

Developed countries, including high-income ones like Singapore, should set ambitious targets for reducing poverty. There is probably very little absolute poverty in Singapore. Nonetheless, it is important that the wage gap between those at the lower deciles of the income distribution and the median wage earner is not unduly large. I will come back to this important theme in my third lecture.

Middle-Class Stagnation

A thriving middle class is a necessary condition for the stability of society and durability of democracy. The gradual erosion of trust in the economic and political system that we see in many advanced economies is due not so much to the widening gap between the rich and the poor but to the stagnation of the middle. Some estimates suggest that there has been hardly any increase in real median wages in the US since the mid-1970s.[20] In the United Kingdom, there has been similar stagnation.[21]

Focusing on the divergent demands for various mid-level skills is more insightful than merely looking at income deciles. There are important differences within the mid-wage brackets that we should recognise. What has been declining in many advanced economies is the traditional middle of the job market, composed primarily of construction, production and clerical jobs that do not require high degree of skills. In the US, the secular decline in manufacturing employment due to technological change has been associated with wage stagnation in the middle.[22] But demand for another set of mid-level skills is growing, in areas such as healthcare, education, mechanical maintenance and repair, and some high-touch social, recreational and community services.

Singapore's experience with median wages has not been bad. Real median wages increased by an average 2.6 per cent per annum from 2011 to 2020, higher than the 1.2 per cent annual growth between 2001 and 2010.[23] Sustaining healthy growth in median wages through active labour market policies will be important to give the broad middle of society hope and confidence in the future. I will speak more about this in my third lecture.

Growing Wealth Gap

Wealth inequality has most likely worsened more than income inequality. According to British economist Lord Adair Turner, average wealth-to-income ratios have gone from around 300 to 400 per cent in 1970 to about 600 per cent in 2014; it must be even higher now.[24] According to the Global

Wealth Report, millionaires make up 1 per cent of the global adult population but account for 43 per cent of global net worth.[25]

Wealth inequality is more pernicious than income inequality. If wealth were merely the accumulation of savings from income, then inequalities in wealth would largely reflect inequalities in income. The work of Thomas Piketty suggests that there has been a lot of wealth accumulation without any significant increase in saving.[26] This is because the prices of assets that form wealth have risen faster than the prices of current goods and services that enter income.

The key driver of wealth inequality in many countries is the rising price of urban land. According to Lord Turner, real estate has grown significantly as a source of wealth in the last 40 years, accounting for more than half of all national wealth in the UK and France. In both countries, the increase in the wealth-to-income ratio over the last 40 years has been significantly driven by the rise in real estate values or property prices.[27]

Property price increases are driven by both consumption and investment demand. As their incomes rise, people devote an increasing percentage of their disposable income to purchases of property in so-called prime locations, which are limited in supply. Over time, this tends to lead to house prices rising faster than incomes. This in turn stimulates investment demand for housing in the pursuit of capital gains. Globally, property has become an investment asset class. Getting on the housing escalator to get rich has become a trend across the major urban centres of the world: London, Sydney, Vancouver, Los Angeles, Dubai, Hong Kong, Singapore and many more.

In almost all societies, wealth is far more unequally distributed than income. As the ratio of wealth becomes more important relative to income, income inequality further increases. Market processes are allocating an increasing share of national income to income from property and other financial assets, and a reducing share to income from work. This is a development that we should be deeply concerned about. I will offer some thoughts on this from the Singapore perspective in my third lecture.

Reduced Social Mobility

Rising income inequality can lead to reduced social mobility. The evidence is rather mixed on whether income inequality has directly reduced social mobility. On the other hand, income inequality has very likely increased disparities in health, education, skills levels and subsequent labour mobility — all of which have an impact on social mobility. A highly skewed income distribution could translate into less equality of opportunity for the next generation. This seems to be happening. Among the rich nations for which studies have been done, those with greater income inequality tend to have less mobility across generations.[28]

We must avoid the risk of a hereditary meritocracy. The word *meritocracy* was coined in the 1950s by Michael Young, a British sociologist. Even then, Young had warned that the incipient meritocracy to which he had given a name could be as narrow and pernicious, in its own way, as the aristocracies of old. The condition of one's birth should not overly determine the outcome of one's life.

The paradox at the heart of the new meritocracy is that how far one goes in education determines how far one goes in life. According to Claudia Goldin and Lawrence Katz from Harvard University, differences in educational attainment explain 60 per cent of America's widening wage inequality between 1973 and 2005.[29] This was attributed to the rising wage premium on education and the soaring cost of college education in America. In short, income inequality is being driven by inequality in human capital.

As the importance of human capital grows, meritocracy itself is at risk of becoming heritable, where the elite reproduce themselves. People are naturally good — some would say biologically programmed — at passing on their privileges to their children. According to Sean Reardon of Stanford University, recent decades have seen a growing correlation between parental income and children's test scores.[30] Educated and successful men and women tend to marry one another. Such assortative mating increases inequality by 25 per cent by one estimate.[31] Such couples typically enjoy two large incomes, provide stable homes for their children, and stimulate them relentlessly from birth with enrichment classes.

Public policies can play a key role in mitigating the adverse effects of income inequality. The key measures are well documented in studies by the International Monetary Fund (IMF) and Organisation for Economic Co-operation and Development (OECD): improving education and skills training; improving access to healthcare; higher infrastructure investment; expanding financial inclusion; increasing labour market flexibility and mobility; and encouraging participation in labour markets across genders and age. These are essentially what Singapore has been doing, with a fair degree of success. But with the acceleration of technological change, labour markets will need to be even more dynamic and flexible, characterised by a high degree of job destruction, creation and mobility. This will probably require more protection and security for workers than we currently have in Singapore. I will touch on this in my third lecture.

The choice is not between growth and distribution. Some people believe that rapid economic growth has been one of the causes of inequality. The reality is that lower economic growth will not improve inequality and will only make redistribution more difficult. Faster growth per se does not create inequality. It is the singular pursuit of growth unaccompanied by measures to facilitate a more even distribution of its benefits that worsens inequality. Such growth will eventually prove unsustainable if a large segment of the society feels left behind. Likewise, carefully designed policies to reduce inequality will not necessarily reduce growth.

The Third Horseman: Technology

The third horseman — Technology — is the fastest. He is galloping way ahead of the others.

I think the four general-purpose technologies that could have the biggest impact are: artificial intelligence (AI), robotics, the Internet of Things (IoT) and blockchains.

Probably the most impactful will be AI — algorithms that are designed to continuously learn from the data that they gather and be able to programme themselves to perform new tasks. AI is being used to process vast quantities of data and recognise patterns. Computers using AI are trading financial assets and operating motor vehicles; they are even writing clean prose and composing music.

Robots are gaining the dexterity to do complex manual jobs. There are robots that are now able to stitch back together a sliced grape or de-bone a chicken wing; these technologies are already being used to perform delicate surgery.

Internet of Things is already ubiquitous. We see it most commonly in the form of mobile phones. They are essentially devices embedded with sensors or software to connect with other systems and devices. Data from IoT devices is making possible the real-time tracking of goods along supply chains and the continuous management of risk in financial services. The potential of IoT devices will increase dramatically as 5G networks and edge computing capacity pick up over the next decade. As more industries become IoT-enabled, new business models will emerge.

Blockchains are still nascent but have transformative potential if they can be scaled. Public blockchains are already being used to coordinate inter-company processes. They may have the potential to enable digitised economic and financial transactions across the world, 24/7, in real time. Exchange of value can be as seamless as sending an email. Tokenisation — representing an asset through a smart contract on a blockchain — can make possible the monetisation of many assets whose economic value is currently unrealised, such as unused file storage, computing power and energy credits. This can unlock latent capacity in the real economy.

A digital economy is emerging and data is its lifeblood. The application of these various technologies is bringing about digitalisation. Over the 2010s, the accumulated universe of data surged from about 1 trillion gigabytes to nearly 50 trillion. According to McKinsey Global Institute, data flows account for about 3.5 per cent of world gross domestic product (GDP).[32] The growth in computational power and vast increase in the volume of data available has enabled data-driven decision-making, using granular, real-time data, including unstructured information, such as social media postings. Driven by consumer demand and innovative firms, digital connectivity seems likely to accelerate, further enhancing the centrality of data to social and economic life.

The COVID-19 pandemic has given a significant boost to digitalisation. Many more people are now comfortable with digital interactions, and remote working models are proliferating. The pandemic has also provided an added reason for digitalisation — resilience. Having a digital backup in case human mobility or physical contact is restricted has become a key feature of business continuity planning.

Digitalisation has, on balance, been democratising. Yes, there is a digital divide between those who have access to digital technology and those who do not. But on balance, digital technology has probably enabled more inclusion than it has created exclusion. The beauty of digital technology is its ease of access through the mobile phone, the Internet and broadband connectivity. There were 2.5 billion smartphone users in the world in 2016; as of 2020, that number has jumped to 3.8 billion.[33] Online digital platforms provide access to the smallest as well as the biggest players; they allow upstarts to build business models with global scale.

Notwithstanding the substantial benefits, the social license for continued digitalisation will depend on how countries address three issues relating to technology: *the data dilemma, cyber threats* and *the impact on jobs.*

The Data Dilemma

The aggregation and extensive mining of data have promoted economic inclusion and opportunity. Firms are able to better understand their customers, deliver more customised services at lower costs and reach out to previously underserved customers.

But this data revolution is being propelled by a handful of digital giants with monopoly powers. A small group of American and Chinese software companies, such as Alibaba, Amazon, Google, Facebook and Tencent, have leveraged first-mover advantages and network effects to become the monopoly facilitators of data flows. Their ability to gather huge amounts of data through their pervasive platforms and to control this data has created an entry barrier for potential competition. They have considerable influence on society through their control of the platforms on which people and firms interact with one another.

This then is the data dilemma: how do we harness the benefits of data aggregation while ensuring a competitive playing field and that individuals' personal data are not misused?

Countries that get their data policies right are better placed to grow the digital economy. This means implementing sensible data governance policies that protect personal data while not impeding innovation and inclusion. Data aggregators should adopt the principles of transparency, fairness and accountability in the use of data. The growing Web 3.0 movement has already seen the private sector create platforms that enable more open and equitable access to data.

Control over data and digital platforms has also become a subject of contestation among nation states. Many developed countries are seeking to tax cross-border digital transactions; many developing countries are imposing data localisation requirements that prohibit the cross-border transfer of data. Excessively taxing digital transactions or prohibiting the sharing of data will increase business costs, reduce efficiency and curtail firms' ability to serve their customers better.

What we need more is data connectivity, not data localisation. In the digital economy of the future, data connectivity agreements among countries will become as important as today's free trade agreements. Singapore is off the starting block, initiating digital connectivity agreements with some like-minded jurisdictions. These could become pathfinders for broader international data agreements. I will elaborate on digital infrastructure and connectivity in my next lecture.

The world needs a new Digital Bretton Woods. Just as the rules for international trade and finance were set by the Bretton Woods agreements following the Second World War, we may need a new set of global rules to govern international data flows and exercise oversight of data monopolies. This will help to provide the foundation for a sound and vibrant global digital economy.

Cyber Threats

The incidence, scale and complexity of cyberattacks have been on a growing trend. Recent attacks on major organisations globally such as Colonial Pipeline, SolarWinds and Microsoft are powerful reminders that the fallout from a cyberattack can be far-reaching. Not content with corrupting a victim's data using crypto-ransomware, cyberattackers are now exfiltrating information from the victim. Cyber criminals are also targeting major third-party information technology (IT) vendors and attacking supply chains to infiltrate the systems of multiple entities.

Breaches in sensitive connected systems can lead to serious consequences. Large-scale cyberattacks that succeed in shutting down the electricity grid, telecommunications network or interbank payment system can have systemic consequences across the economy and society. Critical infrastructure systems are especially at risk from nation states and terrorist groups seeking to obtain classified information or disrupt vital operations.

Digital defence is already a sixth limb of total defence in Singapore. Singapore is in a better place than most countries with a national Cyber Security Agency overseeing a network of sectoral agencies with oversight of the critical infrastructures within their respective sectors. But cyber defence is a work-in-progress. Businesses today are responsible for the security of their premises but they do not take measures to defend themselves against an airborne missile attack from abroad — that is the job of the armed forces. How different from a missile attack is a sophisticated, state-sponsored cyberattack? Should we explore a more integrated cyber defence architecture combining the civilian and the military?

A Digital Bretton Woods could include setting out protocols for behaviour in cyber space. It could also include frameworks for cyber defence, and maybe even rules of cyber engagement. It will not be easy, as nation states themselves engage in cyber espionage and cyberattacks. Is there potential for Singapore, as a trusted, competent and progressive jurisdiction, to play a facilitative role in shaping such an international architecture?

Impact on Jobs

Technology has been changing the nature of work and skills for over 200 years. In the 1750s, the rise of industrial technology devalued the skills of artisans but benefitted millions of less-skilled workers who only had to focus on small portions of an extended process. In the 1980s, IT began to take over medium-skilled work, such as back office jobs. We are now witnessing the advance of technology *across* the skills spectrum: automation for routine work, robotics for manufacturing activities, blockchains for intermediation services, and AI for knowledge work.

The impact of technology on jobs will be uneven across industries. Robotic automation is proliferating in manufacturing, and e-commerce is transforming retail trade. Autonomous vehicles and drones will put at risk jobs linked to driving vehicles to move people or goods. But will there be new jobs to complement or service the robot economy? Or will robots repair robots? We don't know.

With growing automation, we should think tasks not jobs, skills not occupations. Historically, what technology displaces is not jobs and occupations per se but tasks and skills. The introduction of the printing press reduced the value of scribing skills but increased the value of publishing and dissemination skills. The advent of the internal combustion engine eroded the value of horsemanship skills but created value for driving skills. Today, the emergence of search engines is shifting value from knowledge-gathering skills to knowledge-application skills. Technology is unlikely to eliminate a large number of jobs; rather, it will affect portions of almost all jobs to a greater or lesser degree, depending on the type of tasks involved in these jobs.

There are sectors with skills requirements that are likely to be affected by technology in a positive way. Jobs where automation is more likely to be human augmenting rather than replacing include those in education and training, human health and social work activities. Such jobs require significant cognitive and social intelligence and a knowledge of human heuristics.

Reducing the need for human labour is not entirely a bad thing, especially in labour-short Singapore. Can robots transform the construction and cleaning industries and reduce Singapore's dependence on foreign labour?

The key to a good outcome for jobs is to intertwine human and technological capabilities. This is of course easier said than done. But the competition from machines has brought to the fore two quintessentially human qualities: *imagination* and *empathy*. When machines can do more of what we do today, we will do in our jobs more of what makes us essentially human: to think and create, to feel and connect.

Creative imagination is likely to remain the preserve of humans for at least quite some time. Computers have started to display signs of creativity. IBM's AI cooking application, Chef Watson, for instance, reads thousands of existing recipes, and is trained to create combinations that people are likely to find delicious but do not know about.[34] But while computers can come up with novel answers that humans cannot, they still operate in a fixed domain, solving defined problems. In practice, problems change as we try to solve them. To ask new questions or regard old problems from a different angle, the human imagination still has a distinct advantage.

Humans are social creatures, capable of empathy. Although robots are starting to understand human emotions through facial expressions, they cannot offer the deep interpersonal connections that we crave. There will still be a premium placed on hearing our diagnoses from a doctor, even if a computer supplied it, simply because we want to talk about it with another human. As mechanical tasks and even some cognitive tasks become commoditised, perhaps the scarcest resource will be relationship workers — those who excel in building bridges with others. Computers cannot weigh ethical dilemmas and grey areas. On such matters, humans have to remain at the centre of accountability.

Human imagination, empathy and accountability cannot be automated away. In an almost ironic way, technology may well help to make us more conscious of what it means to be human and make us better human beings.

When nothing is certain, everything is possible. Technology will disrupt our familiar ways. But individuals and businesses, facilitated by sound public policies, need to face this challenge not with anxiety but a sense of adventure. I will share my thoughts in the next lecture on how we might do this in a digital economy.

The Fourth Horseman: Climate Change

Of the four horsemen, Climate is the one that poses an existential challenge. He is the most complex and his trajectory is highly uncertain and difficult to assess.

Climate change is already happening. Atmospheric concentrations of carbon dioxide have reached the highest levels in 800,000 years.[35] Over the last three decades, the number of climate-related disasters has tripled.[36] Global sea levels have risen 20 centimetres over the past century, with the rate of increase doubling in the past two decades.[37] The increase in global average temperatures has already reached 1 degree Celsius above pre-industrial levels.[38] Extrapolating current trends in greenhouse gas emissions, global temperatures are expected to rise by over 3 degrees Celsius above pre-industrial levels by 2100.[39] In fact, we may have already crossed some climate tipping points that could trigger self-perpetuating loops and unleash a domino impact.

If the current emissions trajectory continues, the world will most likely experience climate catastrophe. The damage to human and natural systems will be severe and likely irreversible. This includes rising sea levels, frequent natural disasters, extreme wet and dry seasons, higher incidence of vector-borne diseases, decline in food supplies and reduction of biodiversity. According to the Network of Central Banks and Supervisors for Greening the Financial System, global GDP could be 15 to 25 per cent lower by 2100 due to these impacts.[40]

How the world responds to the climate challenge will determine the future of generations to come. To avoid the most severe effects of climate change, global greenhouse gas emissions must come down 45 per cent by 2030 and reach net zero around 2050 to keep global warming to within 1.5 degrees Celsius above pre-industrial levels.[41] This is what 195 countries resolved to do as part of the Paris Agreement in 2016.

There is a renewed sense of urgency and commitment to the climate agenda. Despite the COVID-19 pandemic, 2020 witnessed an unprecedented number of commitments to carbon neutrality and net zero emissions — by governments, corporations and other institutions.[42] Perhaps the pandemic has sensitised us to how closely our lives are intertwined with our environment and how fragile our natural ecosystem is.

Beyond commitments, concerted action is necessary for the world to make the transition to a sustainable future. Long-term ambitions need to be translated into tangible policies and early actions. To reach net zero by 2050, the world needs to start significantly reducing emissions now. The International Energy Authority has released the world's first comprehensive road map on how sectors can transition to a net zero energy system by 2050 while ensuring stable and affordable energy supplies and enabling economic growth.[43]

Singapore is firmly committed to doing its part in the global effort to reduce greenhouse gas emissions. Earlier this year, the government launched the *Singapore Green Plan*, which sets out a road map towards sustainable development, a green economy and net zero emissions. Singapore aims to peak carbon emissions around 2030 and to achieve net zero as soon as viable after 2050. We may need to raise our climate ambition in the coming years.

Climate change presents physical and transition risks to economies and societies. Physical risk arises from the impact of climate-related natural catastrophes and widespread environmental degradation. Transition risks arise from the process of adjustment to an environmentally sustainable economy, including changes in public policies, technological developments in renewable energy, and shifts in consumer and investor preferences. Increases in carbon prices and an energy reset towards renewables are likely to be among the more impactful developments.

Physical Impact

The physical impact of climate change is likely to be multi-directional and varied across regions. Wet places are likely to become wetter and dry places drier. Tropical countries are expected to experience the most severe impacts of climate change. At the same time, rising temperatures in the polar regions of the world could have potentially devastating consequences for sensitive ecosystems across the planet. The distribution of arable land, freshwater resources, and land and sea connectivity, could potentially be altered.

The speed, scale and impact of global warming are highly uncertain. This reflects the complexity of the climate system and its interactions with humanity. In fact, some scientists believe that global warming may well usher in a new Ice Age.[44] The melting of polar glaciers will not only raise sea levels but also reduce the salinity of the oceans that could, in turn, lead to changes in the patterns of ocean currents. If the Gulf Stream, which circulates warm waters across the North Atlantic Ocean, stops functioning, parts of Western Europe and the east coast of the US and Canada could potentially experience Arctic conditions.[45]

As a low-lying tropical island, Singapore is at significant physical risk from climate change. With most of the country lying just 15 metres above sea level, the risk of coastal inundation and inland flooding is real. According to the Centre for Climate Research Singapore, by the end of the century, daily mean temperatures will increase by 1.4 to 4.6 degrees Celsius and mean sea levels will rise by 0.25 to 0.76 metres.[46] To mitigate some of these impacts, we have begun to take measures such as using technology to reduce urban heat, diversifying our water supply in case of dry spells, and building polders to protect our coastline against sea level rise.

Carbon Prices

Carbon pricing is gaining momentum. There are 64 carbon pricing initiatives in the world today, with 35 of them being carbon taxes and 29 emissions trading systems.[47] Today, most of the jurisdictions that have implemented carbon pricing have carbon prices below US$50 per tonne of carbon dioxide equivalent, with the exception of the Scandinavian countries.[48]

However, to put the world on a trajectory towards achieving the Paris Agreement goals, carbon prices will need to be much higher. According to the High-Level Commission on Carbon Prices, led by economists Joseph Stiglitz and Nicholas Stern, and recent estimates by the Network for Greening the Financial System, carbon prices need to increase to between US$100 and US$160 per tonne of carbon dioxide equivalent by 2030.[49] Recently, IMF staff proposed a three-tier carbon price floor among the largest emitters in the world at US$25, US$50 and US$75 per tonne.[50] If large emitters agree on a global minimum carbon price, there is likely to be a convergence globally towards that price. Carbon-intensive exports from countries with lower carbon prices may be subject to carbon border adjustments in importing countries with higher carbon prices.

Singapore is the first country in Southeast Asia to implement a carbon tax. But at S$5 or US$3.75 per tonne of greenhouse gas emissions, it is far below what is needed to catalyse carbon mitigation efforts. I will come back to carbon pricing in my second lecture.

Higher carbon prices will have a significant impact on many industries globally. Activities such as power generation from fossil fuels, steel and cement production, and building and construction, will experience outsize impacts given their current reliance on emissions-intensive inputs and processes. In the electric utility sector, for instance, profits at risk could be as much as 90 per cent of margins by 2030.[51] There will be knock-on impacts downstream, as these activities form the basis for a good part of the economy.

Energy Reset

The global transition from hydrocarbons to renewable energy is gaining momentum and is likely to accelerate. The cost of renewable energy has fallen dramatically over the past decade. While fossil fuels remain the dominant source of energy production, the amount of power generated through wind and solar is rapidly catching up to that generated by coal.[52] Coal power plants are being phased out around the world, but oil and natural gas are likely to remain major sources of energy production until 2040.[53]

The energy reset will be particularly challenging for Singapore because our natural endowments disadvantage the harnessing of renewable energy. We do not have the land space necessary to tap on solar or wind energy, or fast-flowing rivers for hydroelectric power. Singapore needs to be highly innovative to overcome these disadvantages. Using our reservoirs, we are opening one of the world's largest floating solar energy systems. We are exploring transmission lines to neighbouring countries to tap on and trade in the renewable energy they produce. We will need many more of such innovations in the years ahead.

Transitioning to a net zero economy also opens up opportunity in the green economy of the future. Countries with the technological capabilities and fiscal resources will be able to seize opportunities brought about by transition. Singapore is well placed to thrive in a green economy, provided we make some bold, decisive moves. I will touch on this in my next lecture.

Singapore will need to make a whole-of-nation effort to make the transition to a sustainable future. In my fourth lecture, I will speak about a vision for an environmentally conscious nation.

The Singapore Synthesis

The four horsemen are riding through Singapore. Many of their adverse effects cannot be avoided. But if we set our minds to it, Singapore has what it takes to mitigate the downsides, seize the opportunities, and create a better world.

Singapore's remarkable development as an economy, as a society, and as a nation, was made possible by a synthesis of an eclectic mix of policies and approaches. As an economy, Singapore has judiciously combined the invisible hand of markets with the enabling hand of the government to deliver First World prosperity. As a society, it has enshrined meritocracy as the guiding principle while achieving considerable equality in educational and economic opportunity. As a nation, it has been one of the most international in orientation while assiduously building a distinct national identity and ethos.

There has been an overall coherence across policies, a synergy across the various parts: the Singapore Synthesis. Three attributes form the cornerstone of the Singapore Synthesis:

- Adaptation — an ability to adopt best practices from around the world
- Competition — an emphasis on letting the market determine outcomes
- Pragmatism — a focus on what works in practice rather than in principle

These attributes have been decisive in Singapore's success to date and will remain critical for Singapore's future in the face of the four horsemen. But they may not be enough. Adaptation without innovation descends into stagnation. Competition without inclusion degenerates into elitism. Pragmatism without inspiration deteriorates into expediency. We need a refreshed Singapore Synthesis, not replacing but enhancing the old Synthesis.

The new Singapore Synthesis must pivot towards more *innovation*, *inclusion*, and *inspiration*. In the face of the challenges posed by the four horsemen, we need to be more of an *innovative economy*, *an inclusive society*, and *an inspiring nation*. They are about how we make a living; how we build a community; how we find our purpose.

I look forward to discussing with you the new Singapore Synthesis over the next three lectures.

Notes

1. Nicky Phillips, "The Coronavirus Is Here to Stay — Here's What That Means," *Nature* 590, no. 7846 (February 18, 2021): 382–84.

2. WHO, "Up to 650 000 People Die of Respiratory Diseases Linked to Seasonal Flu Each Year," December 13, 2017, https://www.who.int/news/item/13-12-2017-up-to-650-000-people-die-of-respiratory-diseases-linked-to-seasonal-flu-each-year.

3. Tze Pin Ng et al., "Influenza in Singapore: Assessing the Burden of Illness in the Community," *Annals of the Academy of Medicine, Singapore* 31, no. 2 (March 2002): 182; Li Wei Ang et al., "Influenza-Associated Hospitalizations, Singapore, 2004–2008 and 2010–2012," *Emerging Infectious Diseases* 20, no. 10 (October 2014): 1655; Angela Chow et al., "Influenza-Associated Deaths in Tropical Singapore," *Emerging Infectious Diseases* 12, no. 1 (January 2006): 118.

4. See, for example, Gypsyamber D'Souza and David Dowdy, "What is Herd Immunity and How Can We Achieve It With COVID-19?" *Johns Hopkins Bloomberg School of Public Health*, April 6, 2021, https://www.jhsph.edu/covid-19/articles/achieving-herd-immunity-with-covid19.html; Nathaniel Weixel, "Fauci: Herd Immunity Could Require 90 Percent of Country to be

Vaccinated," *The Hill*, December 24, 2020, https://thehill.com/policy/healthcare/531611-fauci-herd-immunity-could-require-90-percent-of-country-to-be-vaccinated.

5. See, for example, Elina Pradhan, "Female Education and Childbearing: A Closer Look at the Data," *World Bank Blogs*, November 24, 2015, https://blogs.worldbank.org/health/female-education-and-childbearing-closer-look-data; "A School for Small Families," *The Economist* 430, no. 9128 (February 2, 2019): 56–58.

6. Elizabeth Brainerd, "Can Government Policies Reverse Undesirable Declines in Fertility?" *IZA World of Labor*, May 2014, https://wol.iza.org/uploads/articles/23/pdfs/can-government-policies-reverse-undesirable-declines-in-fertility.pdf.

7. United Nations Department of Economic and Social Affairs (DESA), Population Division, "World Population Prospects 2019: Probabilistic Projections for Total Population," accessed July 5, 2021, https://population.un.org/wpp/Graphs/Probabilistic/POP/TOT/900.

8. United States National Intelligence Council, *Global Trends 2040*, March 2021, https://www.dni.gov/files/ODNI/documents/assessments/GlobalTrends_2040.pdf, 18–19.

9. DESA, Population Division, *World Population Ageing 2019: Highlights* (New York: United Nations, 2019), 11.

10. Ibid.

11. National Population and Talent Division, Singapore Department of Statistics, Ministry of Home Affairs, Immigration & Checkpoints Authority, and Ministry of Manpower, "Population in Brief 2020," September 2020, https://www.strategygroup.gov.sg/files/media-centre/publications/population-in-brief-2020.pdf, 9.

12. DESA, *World Population Ageing 2019*, 33; Singapore Department of Statistics, "Proportion of Elderly Residents (65 Years & Over) Among Resident Population," [1970–2020 data], accessed July 5, 2021, https://www.tablebuilder.singstat.gov.sg/publicfacing/createDataTable.action?refId=14914.

13. Ministry of Health, "Elderly with Mobility Issues," July 5, 2021, https://www.moh.gov.sg/news-highlights/details/elderly-with-mobility-issues#:~:text=With%20an%20ageing%20population%2C%20we,50%2C000%20between%202000%20and%202020.

14. Ryan Nunn and Jay Shambaugh, "Whose Wages are Rising and Why?" *Policy 2020 Brookings*, January 21, 2020, https://www.brookings.edu/policy2020/votervital/whose-wages-are-rising-and-why.

15. Lawrence Mishel and Jori Kandra, "Wages for the Top 1% Skyrocketed 160% Since 1979 while the Share of Wages for the Bottom 90% Shrunk," *Economic Policy Institute,* December 1, 2020, https://www.epi.org/blog/wages-for-the-top-1-skyrocketed-160-since-1979-while-the-share-of-wages-for-the-bottom-90-shrunk-time-to-remake-wage-pattern-with-economic-policies-that-generate-robust-wage-growth-for-vast-majority.

16. "Crony Tigers, Divided Dragons," *The Economist* 405, no. 8806 (October 13, 2012): 15–18.

17. Martin Feldstein, "Reducing Poverty, Not Inequality," *The Public Interest* 137 (Fall 1999): 33.

18. Jeehoon Han, Bruce D. Meyer, and James X. Sullivan, "Real-Time Poverty Estimates during the COVID-19 Pandemic through March 2021," April 14, 2021, https://harris.uchicago.edu/files/monthly_poverty_rates_updated_thru_mar_2021.pdf.

19. Elise Gould and Hilary Wething, "U.S. Poverty Rates Higher, Safety Net Weaker Than in Peer Countries," *Economic Policy Institute,* July 24, 2012, https://www.epi.org/publication/ib339-us-poverty-higher-safety-net-weaker.

20. See, for example, Drew DeSilver, "For Most U.S. Workers, Real Wages Have Barely Budged in Decades," *Pew Research Center*, August 7, 2018, https://www.pewresearch.org/fact-tank/2018/08/07/for-most-us-workers-real-wages-have-barely-budged-for-decades; Max Galka, "Watch What Has Happened to the US Middle Class Since 1970," *World Economic Forum*, April 13, 2017, https://www.weforum.org/agenda/2017/04/watch-what-has-happened-to-the-us-middle-class-since-1970; Elise Gould, "State of Working America Wages 2019," *Economic Policy Institute,* February 20, 2020, https://www.epi.org/publication/swa-wages-2019.

21. Nye Cominetti, "A Record-Breaking Labour Market — But Not All Records Are Welcome," *Resolution Foundation*, February 18, 2020, https://www.resolutionfoundation.org/comment/a-record-breaking-labour-market-but-not-all-records-are-welcome; David Blanchflower and Stephen Machin, "Falling Real Wages," *CentrePiece* 19, no. 1 (Spring 2014): 20.

22. Martin Sandbu, "The Everyone Economy: How to Make Capitalism Work for All," *Financial Times*, July 3, 2020, https://www.ft.com/content/a22d4215-0619-4ad2-9054-3a0765f64620.

23. Nominal wage data is from the Ministry of Manpower's Comprehensive Labour Force Surveys on the Gross Monthly Income from Work (Excluding Employer CPF) of Full-Time Employed Resident Workers. Real wage growth data are MAS staff estimates, obtained from deflating nominal wage growth by All-Items Consumer Price Index (CPI).

24. Adair Turner, "Wealth, Debt, Inequality and Low Interest Rates: Four Big Trends and Some Implications," *Cass Business School*, March 26, 2014, https://www.cass.city.ac.uk/__data/assets/pdf_file/0014/216311/RedingNotes_Lord-Turner-Annual-Address-at-Cass-Business-School-March-26-2014.pdf, 1.

25. Anthony Shorrocks, James Davies, Rodrigo Lluberas, and Credit Suisse Research Institute, "Global Wealth Distribution 2020," in *Global Wealth Report 2021*, June 2021, http://docs.dpaq.de/17706-global-wealth-report-2021-en.pdf, 25.

26. Thomas Piketty, *Capital in the Twenty-First Century*, trans. Arthur Goldhammer (Massachusetts: Harvard University Press, 2014), 219–220.

27. Turner, *Cass Business School*, 11.

28. See, for example, Miles Corak, "Income Inequality, Equality of Opportunity, and Intergenerational Mobility," *Journal of Economic Perspectives* 27, no. 3 (Summer 2013), 82.

29. Claudia Goldin and Lawrence F. Katz, "The Future of Inequality: The Other Reason Education Matters So Much," August 20, 2009, https://dash.harvard.edu/bitstream/handle/1/4341691/GoldenKatz_EdIneq.pdf?sequence=1&isAllowed=y, 1–2.

30. Meeri Kim, "The Link between Children's Academic Achievement and Family Income," *Blog on Learning & Development*, April 13, 2018, https://bold.expert/the-link-between-childrens-academic-achievement-and-family-income.

31. Jeremy Greenwood et al., "Marry Your Like: Assortative Mating and Income Inequality," *The American Economic Review* 104, no. 5 (May 2014): 351.

32. Jacques Bughin and Susan Lund, "The Ascendancy of International Data Flows," *McKinsey Global Institute*, January 9, 2017, https://www.mckinsey.com/mgi/overview/in-the-news/the-ascendancy-of-international-data-flows#.

33. Bankmycell, "Number of Smartphones & Mobile Phone Users Worldwide," [2016–2021 data], accessed July 5, 2021, https://www.bankmycell.com/blog/how-many-phones-are-in-the-world.

34. Richard Brandt, "What's Cooking Chef Watson?" *IBM*, June 6, 2017, https://www.ibm.com/blogs/think/nl-en/2017/06/06/whats-cooking-chef-watson; Alexandra Kleeman, "Cooking with Chef Watson, I.B.M.'s Artificial-Intelligence App," *The New Yorker*, November 20, 2016, https://www.newyorker.com/magazine/2016/11/28/cooking-with-chef-watson-ibms-artificial-intelligence-app.

35. Kevin Loria, "CO2 Levels Are at Their Highest in 800,000 Years," *World Economic Forum*, May 9, 2018, https://www.weforum.org/agenda/2018/05/earth-just-hit-a-terrifying-milestone-for-the-first-time-in-more-than-800-000-years.

36. OXFAM International, "5 Natural Disasters that Beg for Climate Action," accessed July 5, 2021, https://www.oxfam.org/en/5-natural-disasters-beg-climate-action.

37. Rebecca Lindsey, "Climate Change: Global Sea Level," *NOAA Climate.gov*, January 25, 2021, https://www.climate.gov/news-features/understanding-climate/climate-change-global-sea-level.

38. Met Office, United Kingdom, "Global Climate in Context as the World Approaches 1°C Above Pre-Industrial for the First Time," November 2015, https://www.metoffice.gov.uk/research/news/2015/global-average-temperature-2015.

39. Jeff Tollefson, "How Hot Will Earth Get By 2100?" *Nature* 580, no. 7804 (April 23, 2020): 444–46; Climate Action Tracker, "Global Temperatures: 2100 Warming Projections," [1990–2100 data], accessed July 5, 2021, https://climateactiontracker.org/global/temperatures.

40. Central Banks and Supervisors Network for Greening the Financial System (NGFS), "NGFS Climate Scenarios for Central Banks and Supervisors," June 2020, https://www.ngfs.net/sites/default/files/medias/documents/820184_ngfs_scenarios_final_version_v6.pdf, 8.

41. Megan Rowling, "'Net-Zero' Emissions: What Is It and Why Does It Matter So Much?" *World Economic Forum*, September 23, 2020, https://www.weforum.org/agenda/2020/09/carbon-emissions-net-zero-global-warming-climate-change; Nina Chestney and Jane Chung, "Temperatures to Rise 1.5 Degrees Celsius by 2030–2052 Without Rapid Steps — U.N. Report," *Reuters*, October 8, 2018, https://www.reuters.com/article/idUSL8N1WM0JJ.

42. Michael Holder, "'Unusually Positive News': Does 2020 Mark a Turning Point for Delivering on the Paris Agreement Goals?" *BusinessGreen*, December 2, 2020, https://www.businessgreen.com/analysis/4024335/unusually-positive-news-2020-mark-point-delivering-paris-agreement-goals; United Nations, "LIVE: Climate Ambition Summit," *UN News*, December 12, 2020, https://news.un.org/en/story/2020/12/1079862.

43. International Energy Agency, "Net Zero by 2050: A Roadmap for the Global Energy Sector," May 2021, https://www.iea.org/reports/net-zero-by-2050.

44. See, for example, William H. Calvin, "The Great Climate Flip-Flop," *The Atlantic* 281, no. 1 (January 1998): 59.

45. Renee Cho, "Could Climate Change Shut Down the Gulf Stream?" *State of the Planet*, June 6, 2017, https://news.climate.columbia.edu/2017/06/06/could-climate-change-shut-down-the-gulf-stream.

46. National Climate Change Secretariat, "Singapore's Climate Action Plan: Take Action Today, For a Carbon-Efficient Singapore," 2016, https://www.nccs.gov.sg/docs/default-source/publications/take-action-today-for-a-carbon-efficient-singapore.pdf, 4.

47. World Bank, "Carbon Pricing Dashboard: Map & Data," [2021 data], accessed July 5, 2021, https://carbonpricingdashboard.worldbank.org/map_data.

48. Ibid.

49. Carbon Pricing Leadership Coalition, "Report of the High-Level Commission on Carbon Prices," May 29, 2017, https://static1.squarespace.com/static/54ff9c5ce4b0a53decccfb4c/t/59b7f2409f8dce5316811916/1505227332748/Carbon Pricing_FullReport.pdf, 3; NGFS, "NGFS Climate Scenarios," 15.

50. Ian Parry, Simon Black, and James Roaf, "Proposal for an International Carbon Price Floor among Large Emitters," *International Monetary Fund*, June 2021, https://www.imf.org/en/Publications/staff-climate-notes/Issues/2021/06/15/Proposal-for-an-International-Carbon-Price-Floor-Among-Large-Emitters-460468, 11.

51. Madeleine Cuff, "Report: Why the Auto, Chemical and Electricity Sectors are in Line for a Carbon Pricing Shock," *BusinessGreen*, January 22, 2018, https://www.businessgreen.com/news-analysis/3024826/report-why-the-auto-chemical-and-electricity-sectors-are-in-line-for-a-carbon-pricing-shock.

52. International Renewable Energy Agency, "Renewable Capacity Statistics 2021," March 2021, https://www.irena.org/publications/2021/March/Renewable-Capacity-Statistics-2021, Foreword, 13, 20.

53. U.S. Energy Information Administration, "U.S. Energy Information Administration's International Energy Outlook 2020 (IEO2020)," October 14, 2020, https://www.eia.gov/outlooks/ieo/pdf/ieo2020.pdf, 4.

Question-and-Answer Session

Moderated by Professor Danny Quah

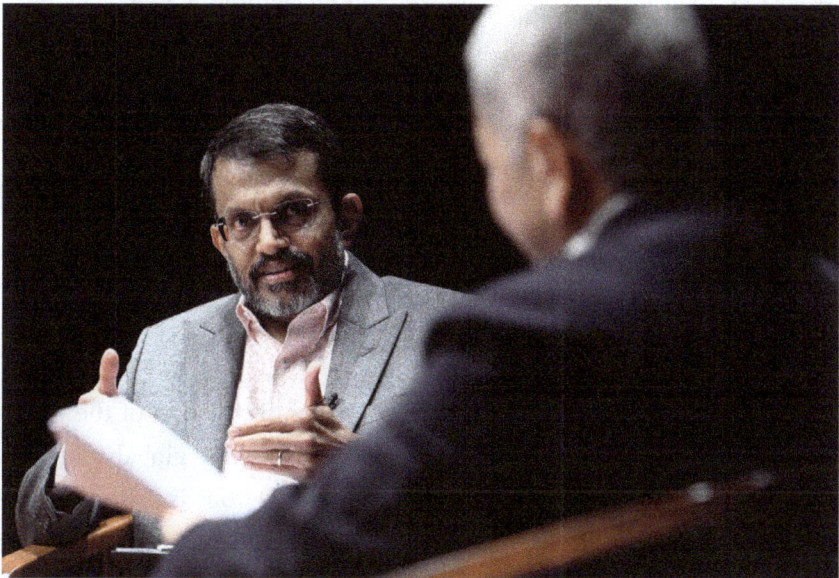

Mr Ravi Menon speaking with Professor Danny Quah at his Q&A session
Source: Jacky Ho for the Institute of Policy Studies

Professor Danny Quah: Good afternoon. I am sure I echo the audience in thanking and congratulating you on such an insightful and wide-ranging lecture — really a tour de force. What I'd like to do is to engage you in a conversation on some of what I thought to be common points across the entire lecture. One of the things that struck me as I listened to you was how there were common patterns across the problems presented to us by "the four horsemen," including the complementary fifth horseman.

One common factor is that these are problems common to many nations. They are pronounced in Singapore, given the characteristics that we have here, but they are challenges all nations face. On top of that, these are not just shared problems but are also interconnected across nations. Climate change, for instance, is the leading example — it is *global climate change*, not American climate change or Singaporean climate change.

An important part of the thinking here is that what happens in one nation spills over into another. This is what economists call externalities. As we wait to hear from you in your remaining lectures on how Singapore takes on its specific challenges, I thought here we could try to get your views on what it means to build international collaboration, going beyond what is specific to Singapore. Your perspective as a central banker, in particular, gives us interesting insight on international collaboration. That insight applies as well to these challenges we are now discussing. Could I get some of your thoughts on building international architectures and the role that Singapore might play facilitating these constructions? What do we need to do as a world going forward?

Mr Ravi Menon: Thank you, Danny. You have hit the nub of the issue. These are global problems, and global problems require global solutions and global actions. The interdependence of our actions is critical to the solution.

During the post–World War period — and I refer to the Bretton Woods system from 1946 — because of the devastation and ravages of war, countries were knocked to their senses and said we should not do this again. They agreed to put in place structures to make the global system naturally cooperative with a way to resolve differences. This resolve was particularly strong in Europe, whereas you know, European nations have been battering one another for 2,000 years; and now, since the Second World War, they've been the most peaceful continent. The rule setting was amazingly visionary with strong leadership from across the world to set up the Bretton Woods Institutions. The General Agreement on Tariffs and Trade modulated trade and the World Trade Organization (WTO), of course, came much later as an institution; the IMF set rules for capital flows and international finance;

and the World Bank was charged with uplifting poor countries from poverty and providing development assistance. This global architecture worked wonderfully well for about 50 years. Today, these institutions are fraying at the edges. There has not been a fresh imagination.

But there are small signs of hope, and I'll just mention a few. One is the Paris Agreement itself. This had been discussed for many years before but came to fruition just recently because nations realised that if we cannot do this together, it is not going to get done because none of us is going to do this on our own. The realisation that this was a classic tragedy of the commons was strong, and the agreement was signed. Now there are commitments being made and strengthened to reduce carbon emissions. We still have to see implementation and action, but at least the commitments are a good sign.

Another good sign was in the immediate aftermath of the 2008 global financial crisis when the world's central banking and financial regulatory community got together and decided this must never happen again: we must end the "too big to fail" problem and strengthen the banking system. We cannot be in a competitive mode to ease standards but must jointly agree on the minimum standards that we are going to set, and we will all follow these rules, even if we are not satisfied with specific parts of the package. That was a huge and highly successful endeavour in international cooperation with all the major countries coming on board.

We need to see some of this global cooperation in the digital arena. I spoke about a Digital Bretton Woods, and there are conversations on digital connectivity going on bilaterally. A lot will depend on leadership shown by the major powers. If this is something that the US, the European Union (EU), China, Japan and others put their minds to, it can happen the way Bretton Woods happened in 1945 and 1946. Are we there yet? Not on every issue. My hope is that we can continue to push the agenda on climate change, because the tensions there are not competitive. All of us are going to get into huge trouble if we do not address climate change, so we had better work together.

The digital space is a little bit more complicated because of the sensitivities around technology. Making technology interoperable, having data flow seamlessly and securely requires a high degree of trust, which doesn't quite exist today among the major powers. Trust has eroded quite considerably over the last five to 10 years and that's going to be a big challenge. So, it is going to be a mixed picture — on some areas we will move further, on others we will probably get stymied.

Prof Quah: Thank you. It strikes me that your response describes two classes of challenges. One, there is a little bit of a zero-sum game where someone has to give up something for anyone else to get ahead. In that class of challenges, it takes the kind of leadership belonging to a great power to force through something that will then work for everyone. There is a second class of challenges where actually no one needs to lose anything, but instead there is a free-rider problem. Many hold back on doing anything because they reckon others will do the job. Embedded in your answer is the idea that in an earlier age, there was an immediacy and an urgency coming out of the Second World War with the great powers in a good position to craft a new architecture. The world is, as you say, different now and the challenges are different with a mix of zero-sum game and free-rider-type problems.

Perhaps I can press you a little bit on this and it relates to a question that's come in from the viewers. It used to be that leadership was the preserve of a great power. But all of us outside the great powers, including Singapore, are only small nations. Arguably, however, we are the ones who have the democratic voice to try and push forward the vision of a fairer and greener world. The challenge that's been put in one of the questions that's come in is, "How does a small country that is historically so good at doing the things that it's done help convince the rest of the world on best practices for economic or environmental health? How do we change that narrative on the role of small nations in this international architecture?"

Mr Menon: Those are basically the challenges of a multipolar world. When the rules of the game were written in a visionary fashion during post–Second World War, it was a small group of players — white men in smoke-filled rooms who hatched all this together. If you want anything done today, it has to be at least the Group of Twenty (G20). The forum has a mix of countries, and rightly so because they all have legitimate voices with different considerations. There is a sense among many developing countries that the international rules of the game have been written by the predominantly developed countries of the time. The world has changed a lot since then. The setting up of the G20 has been a major advancement — it is no longer just the Group of Seven (G7) nations. A lot of the cooperative actions taking place are now being channelled through the G20, albeit slower because of its heterogeneous composition. What kind of role can Singapore play well? I think the biggest premium we have in the global arena is twofold. One is trust. Second is competence. We have a reputation for thinking through issues carefully and offering rational solutions. Everybody knows that they have to make practical adjustments for political and social considerations, but they know Singapore speaks the voice of reason, be it for climate change, cooperation in technology, and so on.

Because Singapore is so small, we have very little vested interests in many of these issues. We can be a facilitator and we have been a facilitator in many things, especially in the old days of the WTO. I think we are beginning to play a bigger role in digital matters by exercising thought leadership. There is trust, plus we have a regime that emphasises good governance, so I think we can play a role. But as a small country, we are not going to pull off anything on our own. You still need the major powers to be broadly aligned. When they are having difficulty converging, then I think Singapore can play a role. But if they are starting with diametrically different positions, that becomes much more difficult. On climate, I am a bit more hopeful. China, the US and the EU recognise the importance of taking collective action. They differ on burden sharing: these are second- and third-order issues, which are certainly not trivial but are the kinds of things that can be reasoned and talked through. There is no fundamental difference on the need to reduce emissions, and in those areas, I think Singapore can play a role because that is where we come in with our premium on trust and competence.

On technology cooperation, I am not hopeful because it is quite a competitive relationship characterised by distrust. I did not touch on it, but the risk of bifurcation of technology due to a mistrust of using one another's systems, components, software or hardware is real. If systems are not interoperable — like in the old days when the Macintosh was not interoperable with the IBM PC — it is going to be detrimental to the creation of a global digital economy. It will be tough because technology is being seen by both the US and China as the main area of contestation and whoever gains supremacy in technology would have an outsized influence in the rest of the world.

Prof Quah: It's very helpful the way you have carved out these sets of problems, especially framing climate change as an easy win — as we all benefit from tackling it. By working together, we can build trust across nations and potentially help on the competition issue. After all, competition is supposed to be good, it makes all of us perform better except when we think competition undermines someone in a profound way.

This takes me to my question on inequality and views on meritocracy in general. Today, meritocracy is in some circles a flashpoint word, and perhaps it always was, ever since its first satirical published usage by the British practical sociologist Michael Young. There are parts of the world and of society everywhere that consider meritocracy a natural extension of putting forward the best people to do the best things. In some parts of the world still, meritocracy is thought of in terms of providing a level playing field. The best emerge, and there is no ill will towards those who have won. Those who've lost do not try to overturn the outcome of that game. Somehow, though, in the decades since we've been discussing meritocracy, including in Singapore, our understanding of it has transmogrified into hereditary meritocracy, meritocracy entrenching elites, and so on. I worry sometimes that we are losing sight of the merits of meritocracy. I want the best brain surgeon to operate on me when my brain is sick, I do not want just anybody to do that. How do we guarantee that kind of an outcome — where the best emerge to do the jobs they are indeed best at, but still not rule out a fair and equitable society where everybody has opportunity to succeed?

Mr Menon: I am fully with you on that. I think meritocracy remains quite critical to the success of the free enterprise market economy and especially for a small country like Singapore. It must be one of the bedrocks of Singapore, just as the market economy and capitalism is. As you know from history, the market economy has undergone many transformations and has had to reform to rid itself of some of its own excesses so that the system remained viable and fit for purpose. As Karl Marx puts it, the capitalist system sows within itself the seeds of its own destruction. To some extent that is what is happening with meritocracy. It is an ideal that most people would regard as fair but there is something about its workings — just like capitalism — that creates dysfunctionalities and its own undermining.

For example, what do we mean by meritocracy and equal opportunity? Everybody starts off in the race together and the person who trains harder and is faster wins the race. I think everybody sees that as fair. But life is not one race; life is a relay. If you have a 4 × 100 metre relay and the baton gets passed on at different times from the person at the second or third leg of the race, then where is the equality of opportunity as the race goes on and on? You are inheriting advantage and that is counter to meritocracy because it is not based on your own merit but rather the advantage you have acquired that allowed you to have an edge.

It does not mean that there is something wrong with meritocracy per se, but it means that meritocracy needs to adjust itself continuously. Taking a leaf from capitalism, if the capital share of income grows indefinitely and the working class is suppressed, then the system cannot be sustained. That is where you have the response: trade unions, worker rights, the Keynesian revolution, the New Deal in America, the welfare state, and so on. These are adjustments to make capitalism function better; in other words, to legitimise the market economy in the eyes of the people so that they see it as a fair system. I think what is an affront to many is a sense of unfairness about the system. The system has to continually re-tune itself to be seen as fair, and that's what we need to do in meritocracy too. We must never discard meritocracy because once we do that, we're finished. But we need to retool it so that equality of opportunity, while never absolute, is roughly maintained.

Prof Quah: There is a question here about Singapore and inequality in particular. Singapore is a small country with a close-knit circle of business leaders who dominate executive positions in companies in the landscape here. How do the not-so-privileged, but equally educated and capable Singaporeans break this barrier?

Mr Menon: Inequality itself is a by-product of how the economy and society function. If we did not have inequality of outcomes, a lot of us will be unhappy. Let me relate a story: Deputy Prime Minister (DPM) Heng Swee Keat, who is on the MAS board, was having lunch with a few of us at MAS. He was, at the time, the Minister for Education. There were a number of us at the table — mostly young mothers and fathers — talking about the stresses of exams and competition. DPM Heng asked, "Instead of allocating schools so finely on the basis of Primary School Leaving Examination (PSLE) points, why don't we ballot?" Straightaway, everybody objected. You see, they are complaining about the competition and stress, and yet when a balloting system was proposed, which would seem in a way fair, everybody objects. So therein lies the difficulty. We do not like the system, but what is the better solution?

Rather than focus on inequality, we should focus on poverty — those really at the bottom. How are they faring? Are they getting a good enough deal that one would expect in a civilised, prosperous country? Are they being well taken care of? I think that should be the first concern, followed by the welfare of the middle class. The idea that democracy survives on the basis of support from the middle goes back to Aristotle. I mentioned in my lecture that Singapore's real median wage in the last 10 years has gone up 2.6 per cent per annum — it is a very decent real wage increase. It means people's lives are getting better at the broad middle and we must always ensure that remains so. But it is not a given, which is why we need to work hard to make sure we should not have in Singapore what has happened in the US — 20 years of wage stagnation in the middle. It is not an inequality problem per se, it is a problem of middle-class stagnation. If the incomes of the poor stagnate, the state can help them, but the middle is too large. It is fiscally difficult and many in the middle do not want to live on state welfare.

Another issue we should focus on is wealth inequality, which is one of the things that undermines meritocracy itself because the accumulation of wealth can far exceed the differences in income from differences in abilities and performance; this wealth accumulation is due to large increases in the prices of financial assets and real estate. With little effort, one becomes extraordinarily rich. Of course, one is taking an investment risk but the returns for that risk can be huge. Wealth inequality creates a sense of unfairness. I do not think anybody begrudges the high pay of the brain surgeon who is operating on you. What people begrudge is if his children inherit his huge wealth, live a high lifestyle without giving back to society, and behave like an elite — that people would not see as fair. Hereditary meritocracy is probably an extreme way of describing what this might end up as, but it is something we must avoid.

Prof Quah: Thank you for such a wonderful, nuanced and complete answer to this question because you have really shown us how if we are simply fast and loose with our language and with the ideas that we throw around concerning inequality, we have hidden away far deeper problems that can be tackled and addressed by policymakers. I am so looking forward to the rest of your lectures as we unpack all of these issues, because there is going to be lots more to come. Thank you so much for this conversation.

Lecture II
AN INNOVATIVE ECONOMY

T he only way out of our trade-offs and dilemmas is to innovate. In my first lecture, "The Four Horsemen," I outlined the challenges posed by demographics, inequality, technology and climate. Dealing with each of these will require generous doses of innovation.

Innovation at the Heart of the New Economy

In today's lecture, I will focus on what it means to be an innovative economy. The demographics horseman will progressively shrink Singapore's labour force. Our labour force participation rates are now amongst the highest globally; further gains will be limited.

Assuming no net migration and no increase in foreign workers, the overall labour force will decline gradually from next year onwards. This means it can no longer contribute to gross domestic product (GDP) growth. The source of economic growth will then be productivity growth, which in turn depends on the growth in capital-to-labour ratio, growth in human capital, and innovation. Singapore's physical capital intensity and educational attainment levels are already high; there is still room for some more growth, but it will not be much. That leaves innovation as our main source of future growth. Here is where the technology horseman and climate horseman come in: they provide powerful impetus for innovation; new business models, new products and solutions, and new markets.

Singapore is no longer a catch-up economy. Most countries are "catch-up" economies, where growth is more about investing in existing ways of doing things. It is not that there is no innovation in these economies; there is, but it is not the main source of growth. Countries like the United States, the United Kingdom and Germany are mostly frontier economies, where most of the growth comes from innovation. Singapore is increasingly closer to a frontier economy.

If we do not innovate, we will stagnate, especially given our demographic drag. As Philippe Aghion from INSEAD puts it, "Innovation and diffusion of knowledge are at the heart of the growth process". One of Singapore's great strengths is its ability to adapt best practices from elsewhere to our local context. But increasingly, we must now dare to be a first mover, with the full knowledge that we will occasionally fail in some of our endeavours.

Innovation must be at the heart of the new economy. Today, I want to highlight three areas where we can be truly innovative:

- Make our *domestic services exportable*
- Transform our economy to be *digital end-to-end*
- Take the lead in Asia as the *vanguard of a green economy*

I will conclude with why an innovative economy needs a *strong Singaporean core working alongside the best global talents.*

Exportable Domestic Services
A Tale of Two Productivities

First, to be a truly innovative economy, innovation needs to be pervasive. A good place to start would be to look at productivity across different sectors. Let me tell a tale of two productivities.

Singapore's overall productivity performance during the last decade has been impressive. Real value-added per worker (VA) grew at a compounded annual growth rate of 1.6 per cent from 2010 to 2019, up from 1.1 per cent in the preceding decade from 2000 to 2009.[1]

Many analysts seem to not appreciate that Singapore's productivity growth over the past decade was better than most advanced economies at similar levels of per capita income. Singapore does not have a productivity problem at the overall level. Our problem is that productivity levels and growth are highly uneven across sectors.

Singapore has a dual economy: an internationally competitive, highly productive, well-paying tradable sector; and a domestically focused, non-tradable sector with low productivity. By tradable sector, I mean manufacturing, wholesale trade, transport and storage, hotels, information and communications technology (ICT) services, professional services and financial services. Together they account for about 70 per cent of GDP but only about 50 per cent of resident employment.[2] The non-tradable sector includes construction, real estate, retail trade, food services, utilities, rental and leasing, administrative services and other services. The dual productivity shows up in wage differentials. Average resident monthly wages in the tradable sector in 2019 (before the COVID-19 pandemic) were around 60 per cent higher than in the non-tradable sector (Figure 1).[3]

Most of Singapore's productivity growth over the last decade was due to productivity gains within sectors, and mostly within the tradable sector. Shifts in employment between sectors contributed negatively to overall productivity growth. The employment share in less productive domestically-oriented sectors increased at the expense of more productive outward-oriented sectors. This shift effect has improved somewhat in recent years as more productive services sectors, such as financial and ICT, created jobs at a healthy pace. But it is not clear this will continue.

Basically, the trend shift in employment towards sectors with lower productivity and lower growth rates remains a challenge.

Moreover, the productivity and wage gaps between the tradable and non-tradable sectors have widened over the years. The productivity gap

Figure 1.   Singapore Tradable and Non-Tradable Sectors

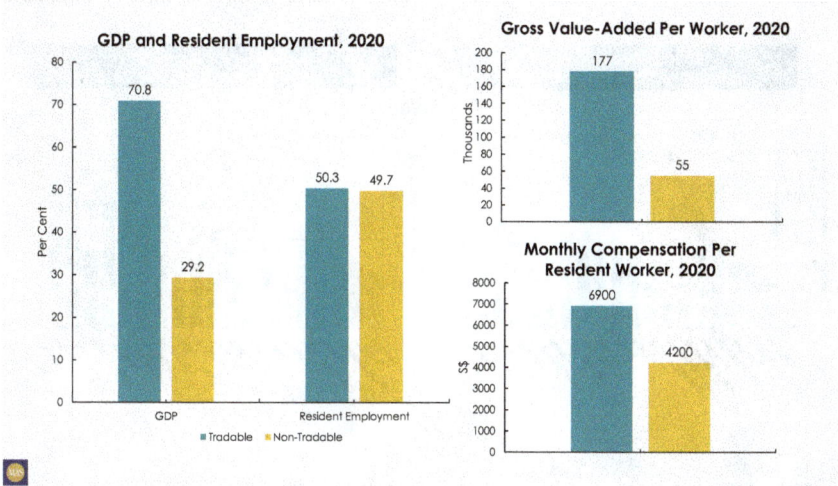

Source: Monetary Authority of Singapore estimates, based on Ministry of Trade and Industry and Ministry of Manpower statistics.

between the sectors has widened from 60 per cent in 2015 to 69 per cent in 2020.[4] So has the wage gap.

The wedge between the tradable and non-tradable sectors is wider in Singapore than international norms (Figure 2). Almost every country has a dual economy structure. But the duality in our economy is more pronounced. It probably reflects the strong outward orientation in our economic development strategies since Independence, while non-tradable services have been hindered by our small domestic market.

It is unlikely that the highly productive export-oriented sectors will be able to significantly raise their employment share. The manufacturing sector has seen weak employment gains since the global financial crisis of 2009 despite strong output growth. Even in recent years, with manufacturing value-added growing by an average of 5.4 per cent per annum from 2016 to 2020, resident employment fell by an average of 1.1 per cent per annum.[5] This secular decline in manufacturing employment has been experienced

Figure 2.   Cross-Country Comparison of Tradable and Non-Tradable Sectors

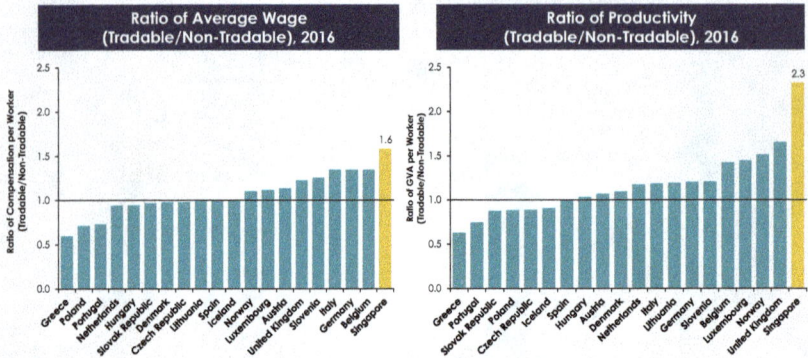

Source: Organisation for Economic Co-operation and Development (OECD); Monetary Authority of Singapore estimates, based on Ministry of Trade and Industry and Ministry of Manpower statistics.

by many advanced economies as well. The financial services sector has done better on the employment front, creating 5,300 net jobs per annum from 2016 to 2020.[6] But these numbers are small compared with the annual supply of Singapore residents entering the workforce, at roughly 24,000 per annum.[7]

We are likely to see continued strong employment growth in some non-tradable domestic services. Some domestic services have high income elasticities of demand, meaning the demand for these services grow faster than growth in incomes — services such as education and continuous training, healthcare, social services, entertainment and recreation. These domestic services are not small. Together they make up 8 per cent of Singapore's GDP, bigger than the banking industry and almost as big as the electronics industry. They account for one out of every seven resident jobs.

We should promote more innovation to increase productivity and wage growth in these domestic services. For a start, we should progressively reduce our reliance on lower-skilled foreign labour in these sectors and allow wages to gradually rise to attract more Singaporeans. This will no doubt imply higher costs, but it could be mitigated in part by a more skilled workforce and higher investment in technology and innovation. Some fiscal support may be necessary to ensure affordability of essential services for lower income households.

The Oxbridge and Mayo of Asia

We should strive to make education and healthcare major exportable services. A large external market will provide the scale necessary to make sizeable investments in technology and human capital, thereby raising productivity and wages.

Can Singapore be the Oxbridge of Asia for education and the Mayo of Asia for healthcare? Given the trust premium Singapore enjoys and the high quality of our education and healthcare systems, coupled with the rise of a more discerning Asian middle class, the stars might be aligned for such a pivot. The key concern in making such a pivot is of course whether the drive to serve overseas customers and raise wages in these sectors will increase education and healthcare costs for Singaporeans. We will need some creative ways to ensure that Singaporeans continue to have access to affordable education and healthcare services.

The export intensity of our education and healthcare services has not improved over the years. In 2017, about 13 per cent of the output in education services was exported, just a tad higher than the 12 per cent in 2010. Meanwhile, the export intensity of healthcare services fell from 15 to 10 per cent during this period.[8] Our export intensity numbers are not bad when compared with many OECD countries, but that is because they have much larger domestic markets to serve. The question for us is this: Should the export intensity of two of our high-quality services sectors that employ a large number of Singaporeans not be even higher?

We cannot hope to be a high-wage, low-cost economy. One man's cost is another man's wage. To escape the dual economy trap, we need to become a high-productivity, high-wage, high-cost economy, where most people can bear the higher costs because they have higher wages, and can earn higher wages because they have higher productivity. There will of course be a group whose wages will not be high enough to bear the higher costs. This is a group whose incomes the state should consider supplementing.

There is somewhat of a fear in Singapore — both among businesses and in government circles — that high wages will translate into a loss of competitiveness. This fear was no doubt implanted deep in our psyche by the shock of the 1985 recession when high labour costs sharply reduced Singapore's international competitiveness. But 35 years later, as a high-productivity economy, that calculus while still relevant is somewhat less compelling. Countries' experiences bear this out. According to the economist Paul De Grauwe, on average, countries with high labour costs are also highly competitive — think of the countries in northern Europe.[9] Likewise, we should aim to create a self-reinforcing virtuous cycle of higher wages and costs accompanied by higher productivity, as well as higher purchasing power and willingness to pay for higher quality domestic services. It will not be easy, and the transition has to be carefully managed. But it is worth trying.

Digital End-to-End

The second key to an innovative economy is to be digital end-to-end. This means two things: digitalising the business processes within a firm end-to-end and ensuring that digital systems across firms are interoperable.

Digitalising only part of a business value chain does little to increase efficiency. Adopting e-payments — while invoicing remains in paper form and reconciliation of accounts requires printing statements — is hardly transformative. Using a digital identity to initiate a transaction but having to provide a wet-ink signature to consummate the deal breaks the digital chain. Digital end-to-end means digitalising every stage of the business value chain, so that the transaction is *paperless* and *presence-less*. The front-end operations of sales, purchases and payments must be fully integrated with the back-end, financial accounting, tax filing, inventory management and supply chain monitoring.

The second gap in the digital economy is the lack of interoperability. Although a variety of digital solutions has proliferated, their services and solutions are often not interoperable. As a result, we are not able to exploit the full efficiency benefits of digitalisation. It also means that the digital economy is not as inclusive as it should be, with users segmented by walled gardens built by providers of digital services.

A comprehensive digital ecosystem is key to creating a truly digital economy. This means collective governance, common standards, open architecture and interoperable infrastructure, so that network effects can be maximised and the full potential of individual innovations realised. We need collaboration across government, industry, research institutions and the technology community at large. The degree of collaboration required is not trivial — which is why few countries are even trying to do this. Singapore is doing this quite systematically and quite well too. But we are not done yet.

Let me elaborate on the four key components of such a digital ecosystem: *digital infrastructure*, *digital governance*, *digital inclusion*, and *digital connectivity*.

Digital Infrastructure

Singapore has put in place the foundational infrastructure for a digital economy. Just as physical infrastructure like railroads helped to advance the industrial economy, digital infrastructure will spur the growth of the digital economy. It allows different users, different solutions and different devices to seamlessly interact with one another. A foundational digital infrastructure enables interoperable solutions and seamless digital services to reach more people and businesses at lower cost and greater convenience. It avoids the pitfalls of isolated technology solutions — *digital islands* and *walled gardens*.

I would describe Singapore's foundational digital infrastructure as comprising four mutually reinforcing layers.

The first layer is the national digital identity in the form of Singpass. A digital identity establishes trust at both ends of the digital interaction. It enables access to the realm of public and private digital services across different sectors; it promotes digital inclusion. Singaporeans can use Singpass to transact digitally with both the government and the private sector. It can be used for authentication, verification and digital signing.

The second layer is trusted and secure data in the form of MyInfo. MyInfo is a government digital service that enables Singapore residents to authorise third parties to access their personal data residing across different government agencies through application programming interfaces (APIs). This means that, with the consent of the customer, banks can use the MyInfo service to obtain government-verified personal data for more efficient Know Your Customer (KYC) processes. Corporate data can be similarly accessed and made available by authorised corporate users through MyInfo Business APIs.

The third layer is an authorisation framework. To foster public confidence that digital transactions are safe and secure, we need mechanisms for consent by individual users or corporate users to ensure that the use of data is properly authorised. These mechanisms also ensure transparency in the use of data — that data will be used and shared in accordance with the purposes for which it has been provided and in a manner that is expected and understood by individuals. Today, using Singpass, Singaporeans can make available relevant verified information from MyInfo to allow banks to onboard them without paper documentation or physical presence.

The fourth layer is an electronic payments rail in the form of FAST and PayNow. FAST is the core backbone — a 24/7 Internet-based payment system that allows us to transfer funds directly from our bank account to another bank account in real time at zero cost. PayNow rides on FAST to allow payments to be made into the payee's bank account using just the payee's mobile number or NRIC. Business users of PayNow can generate a QR code containing their unique entity number. We can pay our utilities provider, telephone company or plumber by simply scanning their QR code using our smartphone and keying in the amount to be transferred. The FAST/PayNow infrastructure has made digital payments interoperable and seamless.

Digital Governance

The second key component of a comprehensive digital ecosystem is governance. Sound digital governance gives space for innovation while giving people the confidence to engage in the digital economy.

First up is smart regulation to mitigate risks while harnessing benefits and not hindering innovation. This means taking a risk-based approach to regulating new technology. Regulators need to keep pace with innovation, but regulation itself must not front-run innovation. Introducing regulation prematurely may stifle innovation and potentially derail the adoption of useful technology. Smart regulation allows experimentation outside the regulatory perimeter but within controlled boundaries through mechanisms like the regulatory sandbox. Regulation should be introduced when the risk posed by the new technology becomes material or crosses a certain threshold.

Second, a sound governance framework for the use of data in a digital economy. Data privacy policies should allow the harnessing of benefits from data aggregation and data sharing while safeguarding confidentiality of personal data. Transparency is one of the key principles for fostering trust in a digital economy. Users and data subjects must be given clear explanations of what data is being used, how it is being used as well as the consequences of decisions made using the data. Singapore has begun to put in place the foundations for a sound data governance framework. The Infocomm Media Development Authority (IMDA)'s Trusted Data Sharing Framework underpinned by the Personal Data Protection Act is a good baseline for data partnerships in a digital economy.

Third, we should seriously consider mandating basic cyber hygiene for all businesses engaged in the digital economy. It is as essential as fire safety requirements. Cyber hygiene includes basic things such as securing administrative accounts, controlling network access at the perimeter, installing security patches promptly, installing antivirus software, data encryption at rest and in transit, monitoring database activity, and multi-factor authentication for users who access confidential information over the Internet. Research shows that more than 80 per cent of cyber incidents could have been avoided if these basic precautions were in place.[10] A smart nation must first be a cyber-secure nation.

Digital Inclusion

A third priority to get right early in the digitalisation journey is digital inclusion. Everyone must have access to a set of basic digital enablers to participate meaningfully in the emerging digital economy. For a digitally integrated and inclusive society, we should aim for every child in Singapore entering secondary school to have a digital identity, a bank account accessible via Singpass, a registration with PayNow and a basic mobile device with Internet capability. There is an opportunity here to integrate Singpass, PayNow, and a basic no-frills bank account, as a *digital enabler package*. Of course, the bank account should be in trust or joint with parents till the child reaches 18 or 21. There are several non-trivial implementation issues to consider but none seems insurmountable.

The most efficient way to enhance the digital inclusion of small and medium-sized enterprises (SMEs) is perhaps through utility-like digital platforms. These are common platforms into which they can plug and play, rather than build a comprehensive, bespoke digital infrastructure for each SME. To reach out to so many SMEs — to get them to build their own proprietary digital capabilities and infrastructure — is going to be hugely difficult. It is better to help them build some basic digital connectivity capabilities and they can then plug into these platforms.

Singapore can become a truly digital economy if we can achieve broad-based SME digitalisation. IMDA is helping SMEs gain access to digital resources under the SMEs Go Digital initiative. SMEs are offered virtual assistance, or Chief Technology Officer-as-a-Service, to help them identify their digitalisation needs and choose the appropriate digital solutions. Enterprise Singapore is engaging SMEs upstream through a Start Digital Pack. The aim is to equip all new businesses at the point of incorporation, with core digital tools such as digital identity, e-payments, e-invoicing, digital accounting, digital marketing and cybersecurity.

Digital Connectivity

The fourth key component of a comprehensive digital ecosystem is digital connectivity. In fact, digital connectivity beyond Singapore will be the most impactful expression of what it means to be an end-to-end digital economy.

Singapore is breaking new ground through a series of digital connectivity initiatives that will position us strongly as an innovative and connected digital economy.

First, seamless cross-border trade through the Networked Trade Platform (NTP). NTP is a one-stop trade and logistics ecosystem that connects players across the trade value chain in Singapore and abroad. All documents are digitised and the process is digitalised end-to-end. NTP functions as several things rolled into one: a trade information management system linked to other systems, a platform offering a range of trade-related services and cross-industry data to gain deeper insights, and a document hub for digitisation at source that enables a single set of data to be used within a streamlined process. The next step is to enable the digital exchange of trade documents with key destination markets. The Ministry of Trade and Industry (MTI) and Singapore Customs are talking to a few countries to explore this.

Second, a one-stop clearance portal for ships calling at the Port of Singapore through digitalPORT@SG. The portal streamlines about 16 regulatory applications that were previously submitted to various agencies such as the Maritime and Port Authority of Singapore (MPA), the Immigration and Checkpoints Authority (ICA) and National Environment Agency (NEA) into a single window for port clearance services. The next phase of the initiative aims to integrate just-in-time and other port services to improve vessel turnaround time.

Third, end-to-end digitalisation of the supply chain through the Singapore Trade Data Exchange (SGTraDex). SGTraDex aims to connect local and global supply chains via a trusted, secure and intuitive data-sharing infrastructure. Through enabling seamless data exchange between supply chain stakeholders, SGTraDex aims to extend Singapore's competitive advantage as a hub for international trade and shipping into the virtual realm. SGTraDex will enable Singapore to offer transparency in documentation, interoperability of trading and shipping systems, and full traceability along supply chains. Transparency and traceability along supply chains are becoming a strong value proposition amidst the rising demand for more stringent environmental, sustainability and governance standards.

Fourth, holistic personal financial planning through the Singapore Financial Data Exchange (SGFinDex). This is a pioneering data exchange platform, the first of its kind in the world, which uses Singpass and a centrally managed online consent system to enable Singaporeans to access their financial information held across different government agencies and financial institutions. Singaporeans can seamlessly consolidate their financial information and use digital tools to make holistic financial planning decisions. The next stage is to include data from the Central Depository as well as data from insurance companies to enable individuals to have a more complete view of their financial status.

Fifth, enhanced access to global customers and suppliers — Business sans Borders (BSB). It is not just cross-border trade that SMEs have to contend with. They have to look abroad for business opportunities for suppliers and customers, as well as to manage procurement and logistics across borders. BSB is designed to connect different platforms globally to help SMEs seamlessly access a much larger ecosystem of buyers, sellers, financiers and logistics providers. It uses artificial intelligence (AI) to enable SMEs to discover prices, diversify sales opportunities, access various supply chains, and source for relevant digital and financial solutions across the BSB network. BSB has just been operationalised by a private commercial entity called Proxtera.

Sixth, aligning digital rules and standards to support cross-border digital trade through Digital Economy Agreements (DEAs). Singapore has pioneered and concluded DEAs with Chile, New Zealand and Australia.

DEAs help to achieve cross-border digital connectivity by aligning digital rules and standards, facilitating interoperability between digital systems, and supporting secure cross-border data flows. They contain provisions for personal data protection, the ethical use of AI, cross-border regulatory sandboxes, interoperable e-invoicing systems, and co-operation towards compatible digital identity regimes. DEAs will enable our businesses to connect digitally with their overseas partners more seamlessly. They will lower operational cost, increase business efficiency and facilitate easier and trusted access to overseas markets.

When we put together these six digital connectivity programmes, it makes for a compelling and powerful digital architecture. Few countries, if any, have such a comprehensive digital ecosystem. It gives Singapore a distinct advantage in the emerging global digital economy.

Vanguard of the Green Economy

The third dimension of an innovative economy is for Singapore to be the vanguard of a green economy revolution in Asia. It entails deep structural reforms to the way our economies operate. The world needs to move away from a resource-intensive economic model of extraction and consumption — essentially unchanged since the Industrial Revolution — towards a 21st century approach of resilience and sustainability, protecting the environment while generating inclusive growth and prosperity.

The green economy is horizontal, not vertical. We sometimes think of the green economy as a sector — a collection of green industries and activities. Rather, a green economy should be viewed as the state of the economy itself. It is like the digital economy I spoke about previously. The digital economy is not the 5 per cent of GDP made up by the ICT services sector but a *horizontal* that cuts across all sectors. The same is with a green economy. It is a theme that cuts across all sectors, it is about greening the economy as a whole.

A green economy is low carbon, resource efficient and socially inclusive. In a green economy, growth in income and employment is driven by investments that reduce greenhouse gas emissions and pollution, enhance energy and resource efficiency, and avoid the loss of biodiversity. The green economy is based on the understanding that the economy depends on the natural environment and the coexistence of people and nature.

A green economy adopts a life cycle approach to minimising environmental footprint. The life cycle of a product transits through raw material extraction, conceptual design, manufacturing, distribution, consumption and end-of-life treatment options such as recycling, recovery and reuse. A life cycle approach allows us to recognise how our choices influence what happens at each stage of production, identify hidden opportunities, and account for unintended consequences and spill-over implications.

An Opportunity Not a Cost

Going green should be seen as an economic opportunity, not a cost. Greening the economy is not necessarily a drag on growth but can potentially be a new engine of growth. Equally important, it can be a net generator of good jobs. According to the International Labour Organization (ILO), the global shift to a green economy could create 24 million new jobs by 2030. At the same time, an estimated 6 million jobs in coal-powered electricity, petroleum extraction and other sectors could disappear by 2030.[11] Many of the new green jobs will require different skills than previous energy jobs or will be in new locations. People who currently depend on fossil fuel-intensive activities need support to thrive in a zero-carbon future.

Like all economic transformations, the green transition will involve winners and losers, and unless this is recognised and dealt with, the sustainability agenda will lose social legitimacy. One dimension of the distributional impact is how households with different income levels are affected. Research has shown that environmental policies in developed countries tend to have regressive effects, with lower-income households being more negatively affected in relative terms.[12]

An efficient yet equitable transition to a green economy requires close consultation and proactive planning among all stakeholders — workers, employers, governments, communities and civil society. This ensures that people who currently depend on fossil fuel-intensive activities receive the support, social protection and investments they need to thrive in a zero-emissions future, and that the costs and benefits of climate action are distributed equitably. According to empirical work by the United Nations Environmental Programme, the greening of economies neither inhibits wealth creation nor employment.[13] However, there is a period of job losses during this transition, which requires investment in reskilling and re-educating the workforce. With adequate planning, dislocated workers can find good jobs in related sectors. For instance, some skills in traditional oil and gas roles are relevant to carbon-capture utilisation and storage, and low-carbon gas production and transport roles.

The transition to green is not without risk, but if well planned and executed, the pay-offs can be substantial. Take, for instance, the contrasting fortunes of two large coal mining regions in the world — the Appalachian region in America and the Ruhr valley in Germany. The mass closures of coal mines in the Appalachian region led to a heartbreaking story of high unemployment, intergenerational poverty and social dysfunction. Similarly, the Ruhr region lost 70 per cent of its 480,000 coal mining jobs over a 25-year period.[14] However, employment in the region eventually recovered as workers found jobs in environmental technology. This successful transition was the result of forward planning, investments in industry diversification, staggering of mine closures, and a comprehensive package of support measures, leading to a restructuring of the regional economy with no job losses.

Singapore should aim to be the vanguard of a green economy revolution in Asia. As a country, we have always been committed to the idea of sustainable development: economic growth with environmental protection and social inclusion. We embedded greenery in our urban landscape. We preserved a small tropical rainforest right in the middle of the city. We were one of the earliest countries in the world to limit our car population. Most of all, we have the ingredients of the success story of the Ruhr region — proactive planning, long-term orientation, tripartite consultation and co-operation. We can not only green our own economy but also contribute to the greening of Asia's economies, creating new business opportunities and jobs.

Going green is a whole-of-economy, whole-of-society effort. The drive towards sustainability will touch almost all aspects of economic and social activity. The changes we need to make and capabilities we need to build are manifold:

- Green technologies to decouple growth from the depletion of natural capital
- Eco-industrial parks to reduce the carbon footprint of production processes
- Procurement practices that take sustainability into consideration
- Capacity building programmes in sustainability for businesses, especially SMEs
- Sustainability skills frameworks for workers
- Eco-labelling to provide consumers information about the environmental impact of the products they purchase, and so on

Let me touch on two critical success factors for a green economy where Singapore needs to considerably step up: *measurement and disclosure* and *carbon pricing*.

Measure and Disclose

A prerequisite for greening the economy is to first measure how brown it is.

To be a credible green economy, our companies must identify, measure and disclose their carbon footprints, set emissions reduction targets and report progress. What gets measured gets managed. We need widespread adoption of standard metrics to measure the carbon footprint of various economic activities, and globally compatible taxonomies to determine what are green, transition and brown activities. Measurements must in turn lead to disclosure that is high-quality and comparable so that sound climate-informed economic and financial decisions can be made.

The availability of trusted sustainability data remains a big challenge. The process of data acquisition is manual, cumbersome and costly. There is also lack of transparency in the verification and reporting process. These challenges are not unique to Singapore, they are universal. But we have an opportunity to be a first-mover solution provider.

Technology can potentially be our game changer in addressing some of these data challenges. To acquire relevant energy consumption data, we can look at solutions like APIs that connect directly to existing systems, Internet of Things (IoT) devices and sensors to measure directly at source carbon emissions, and satellite imagery to track the progress of reforestation and other carbon sequestration projects. To maintain provenance and traceability in the data collected and mitigate the risk of greenwashing, we could look to distributed ledger technology. There are also emerging technology solutions to automatically generate customised and comprehensive environmental impact reports for clients. Many of such experiments and prototyping are already underway in Singapore.

Singapore cannot afford to lag behind international efforts towards a global sustainability reporting standard. The Group of Seven (G7) has expressed support to move towards mandatory climate-related financial disclosures. The G7 has also agreed on the need for a baseline global reporting standard for sustainability that jurisdictions can supplement. Efforts by international standard setters towards a baseline global sustainability reporting standard have gained significant momentum and support. MAS is playing an active role in these international efforts.[15] The key question is whether our companies can step up to the emerging sustainability reporting standards.

MAS and Singapore Exchange (SGX) will set out road maps for mandatory climate-related financial disclosures by financial institutions and listed entities, respectively. The roadmap will take a phased approach.

A more ambitious timeline can be considered for listed entities that are larger or more exposed to climate risks. Larger financial institutions can similarly be prioritised. Details will be worked out in consultation with the industry in the coming months but the key point is that there is not much time to lose.

Carbon Taxes

As I mentioned in my last lecture, carbon pricing is gaining momentum globally. This price can be set either by governments through carbon taxes, or market forces through cap-and-trade systems where market participants can trade their emissions allowances.

A meaningful price for carbon is the cornerstone of a successful transition to a green economy. Without getting the price of carbon right, most sustainability efforts will not make economic sense and thereby not gain traction. The right price of carbon is the social cost it imposes on the environment. As mentioned in my last lecture, estimates of what that price should be in 2030 vary considerably but the lower end of the estimates — at US$75 per tonne of CO_2 equivalent — is above the carbon taxes of most countries.[16] According to the World Bank, less than 5 per cent of the emissions covered by a carbon pricing initiative are priced at a level consistent with achieving the goals of the Paris Agreement, namely, US$40–80 per tonne of CO_2 by 2020 and US$50–90 per tonne of CO_2 by 2030.[17] Among jurisdictions that have introduced a carbon price, Singapore is an outlier at US$3.75.

Carbon taxes in Singapore will have to move to a steeper trajectory to help us meet our climate commitments. The original intention was to gradually raise the carbon tax from 2023 onwards to S$10–15 (about US$7–11) per tonne of CO_2 equivalent by 2030. The government is now reviewing both the post-2023 trajectory and the level of the carbon tax to ensure that they provide sufficient impetus for emissions reduction and restructuring towards a greener economy. Early forward guidance of the future trajectory in carbon taxes will give businesses time to start restructuring towards less carbon intensity and avoid sharper and more painful adjustments later on.

Higher carbon taxes will of course impose a short-term drag on the economy, but fears of a loss of competitiveness are overstated. Empirical work on the European experience over the period 2005–2020 finds no robust evidence of carbon taxes reducing employment or GDP growth.[18] Sweden's experience is illustrative: it is possible to reduce emissions while maintaining economic growth. The Swedish carbon tax is by far the highest in the world today at €114 or US$134 per tonne of CO_2 emitted.[19] During the period between 1990 and 2018, Sweden's GDP increased by 83 per cent, while domestic greenhouse gas emissions decreased by 27 per cent.[20] In 2019, Sweden ranked 8th on the Global Competitiveness Index.[21] Of course, Sweden also had real alternatives to fossil fuels, such as nuclear and hydroelectric power. Singapore does not have these options, so the trade-off will be sharper. But we do not need to go anywhere near a carbon tax of US$100. The important point that these country experiences are conveying is that Singapore can afford significantly higher carbon taxes than currently envisaged and still remain competitive as an economy.

Singapore's approach of starting with a low carbon tax makes sense but only if it increases steadily over time. Economic research has found that carbon pricing that starts at a lower rate and gradually rises until it achieves the intended target is more efficient than a carbon price that remains constant over time.[22] Giving the economy time to adjust to rising carbon prices imposes lower distortionary costs. Once again, Sweden offers a good example. The carbon tax was introduced in 1991 at €23 per tonne and gradually increased over the years to the current €114.

Carbon taxes should be designed equitably. Otherwise, its effects can hit lower-income households hardest. A carbon tax is in a way like the Goods and Services Tax (GST). The fact that the GST is regressive does not make it a bad tax. Singapore has found a novel way of giving GST offsets to lower-income households to mitigate the impact of the GST on them. Similarly, part of the proceeds of carbon taxes could be distributed to lower-income households through carbon dividends. This retains the desired allocative effects of higher carbon taxes while dampening its distributional consequences.

Carbon taxes will have to be complemented by more stringent environmental regulation. Otherwise, the carbon tax would be untenably high, bearing the full burden of effecting the transition towards lower carbon intensity. Stricter environmental regulation will deter environmentally harmful behaviour in the first place so that the carbon tax does not need to do the heavy lifting.

Singaporean Core with Global Talent

Ultimately, to enable the four strategies I have outlined to become an innovative economy, we need a strong Singaporean core working alongside the best of global talents. This means going the extra mile to build a strong Singaporean core to anchor and grow new businesses. It also means remaining open to expertise and skills from abroad that we are in short supply of.

It is gratifying to see more young Singaporeans turning to entrepreneurship. They are working in tech start-ups and acquiring skills in innovation — and lessons in failure — that no multinational corporation (MNC), bank or government agency can provide. It is heart-warming to see local born and bred start-ups succeed, venturing into the region, becoming unicorns, and raising capital in international capital markets. If I have any regrets about my own career, it is that I did not spend a couple of years in a start-up.

By any objective standard, few governments in the world focus as much energy and effort in developing the human capital of their citizens. Singapore has an astonishing array of heavily subsidised training schemes, professional conversion programmes, job attachments, specialist scholarships, leadership development, overseas postings, internships and traineeships. A growing number of firms are tapping these schemes.

Singapore has a fairly open regime in admitting foreigners on employment passes. Being a magnet for talent from around the world has considerably enhanced Singapore's attractiveness as a place to locate high value-added activities. This has in turn generated good jobs for Singaporeans. In this lecture, when I refer to foreigners, I mean those on employment passes, not those on work permits.

This two-pronged talent strategy — of growing a strong Singaporean core and attracting talents from abroad to complement our workforce — is however coming under strain.

Among some segments of the local population, there is growing unhappiness over job competition from foreigners. According to polls by the Ministry of Communications and Information (MCI), a majority of Singaporeans agree that Singapore needs foreigners in our workforce and that they make important contributions to Singapore.[23] But paradoxically, many also feel that foreigners are a threat to their job security.[24] Perhaps what these Singaporeans are saying is: "Foreigners in our workforce are good for the country as a whole but I am concerned about losing my job to a foreigner." This is a perfectly natural and understandable feeling. Job anxiety is also accentuated by the perceived lack of fairness in the hiring and promotion process, with some Singaporeans feeling that many foreign employers hire or promote foreigners on the basis of nationality rather than merit.

At the same time, segments of the expatriate community here have been feeling increasingly unwelcome. The delay in allowing employment passholders and their dependents to return to Singapore during the two phases of heightened alert when our infection numbers were high has caused some understandable distress, especially for families that were separated. Some have been stranded overseas for more than a year. Measures such as freezing the issuance of employment passes for breaches of the Fair Consideration Framework and cancelling the work passes of foreigners who breach safe management measures have had a chilling effect on several MNCs and expatriates. The growing online hostility towards foreigners has also not helped matters.

We need to resolve this affective divide. To be fair, it is nowhere near as bad as in many other countries. We have, through years of hard work, built up a strong base of multiculturalism, tolerance and acceptance. The vast majority of locals and expatriates live and work together in Singapore in harmony. But Singapore cannot afford to be seen either as lacking in opportunity for our own citizens or unwelcoming of foreigners. In today's lecture, I will touch on why this is important for our economy. In my final lecture, I will speak about why this is important for us as a people.

As I mentioned in my first lecture, there is growing interest by global MNCs and financial institutions to invest or expand in Singapore. Our skilful handling of the COVID-19 pandemic, sound approach to policymaking, and progressive stance towards innovation and technology, coupled with heightened uncertainty over global economic conditions, has prompted several international firms to consider rebalancing their regional and global footprint towards Singapore.

The Economic Development Board (EDB) is attracting strong investment commitments to set up cutting-edge manufacturing facilities in Singapore. These include building electric vehicles, producing vaccines and fabricating advanced semiconductor chips. Expertise in automotive engineering, vaccine development and high-end chip design is not widely available here, and so these firms need to be able to bring in experts to complement the Singaporean workforce to enable the ramp-up of production.

There is strong interest among MNCs and global financial institutions to expand their regional headquarters activities here. This will involve the relocation of key decision makers and core teams to Singapore. There are even some companies looking to redomicile and relocate their HQ to Singapore. The agglomeration of HQ functions will help to create many local jobs, but these companies will need to bring their senior management teams to set up and kick-start their operations in Singapore.

There is increased interest from international firms to shift their technology and innovation functions to Singapore. These plans include building up research and engineering teams with manufacturing and product development capabilities. At EDB's urging, many of these manufacturing firms are recruiting fresh graduates from our universities, polytechnics and Institutes of Technical Education (ITEs), but they will need to relocate senior engineers from abroad to support the ramp-up of the new teams and development of local capabilities. Likewise, various financial institutions have designated Singapore as their global IT hub or Asian technology centre. Many of the apex jobs in these centres require deep domain knowledge in areas such as blockchains, cybersecurity, machine learning and cloud computing, where there are not enough Singaporeans. But these apex jobs create many other jobs that provide opportunities for the Singaporean workforce to gain experience and skills in these areas.

Likewise, the four digital banks that MAS has granted licenses to are expected to hire around 1,000 employees over the next three years. They will need to bring in expertise in areas of shortage here, such as software development, data analytics and AI. But MAS will require the digital banks to undertake the transfer of knowledge and skillsets to locals over the initial start-up period, so that the teams will be mostly made up of Singaporeans.

Opportunities like these do not come often. But a key question that many of these firms ask is whether Singapore will remain open to foreign talents.

Singapore's value proposition as an innovative business hub will be at serious risk if we restrict the flow of talent and expertise. A weakening of Singapore's hub status will have adverse medium- to long-term implications, not only for local jobs and wages but also Singapore's standing in the world.

But the anxieties that some Singaporeans feel about the influx of foreigners are real and need to be addressed.

First, the minimum qualifying salary for special pass holders and employment pass holders should continue to be raised over time. The government has progressively raised these qualifying salary thresholds. As Singaporeans continue to attain higher levels of education and acquire deeper specialist skills, they should be able to take on these jobs — provided the wages are higher. Raising wages in the middle of the income distribution is a theme I will touch on in my next lecture. In fact, should we consider raising and pegging the minimum qualifying salary for special pass holders at somewhere closer to the median monthly income (currently about S$4,500)?

We should be cautious though about tightening employment passes at the higher end as that could well lead to loss of adjacent local jobs. An internal MAS study from 2016 shows that there is generally a high degree of complementarity between high-skilled employment passholders and local professionals in the financial services sector. According to an internal MAS report from 2016, there is corroborative evidence from other sectors too that by facilitating business expansion into new areas, high-skilled employment pass holders tend to create employment for locals rather than substitute for them.

Second, we should more directly target the issues relating to discriminatory hiring in favour of foreigners in some firms. The Fair Consideration Framework seeks to ensure that Singaporeans have equal opportunity to fill vacant positions. Today, firms that breach the framework face the prospect of a freeze on their employment pass privileges. But rather than curtail the inflow of foreign workers and thereby restrain business growth and job opportunities for locals, we might want to consider directly punishing the individuals in the firm found to have engaged in discriminatory hiring. Measures could potentially include imposing financial penalties, reducing bonuses and freezing promotions. This will have a strong deterrent effect. Discrimination of any form should have no place in Singapore.

Being an international hub is the only way a small country like Singapore can aspire to First World standards of living. Singapore attained its current level of prosperity by being an international centre tapping international talents and serving an international market. But this also means that we must accept a higher foreign presence in Singapore than is the case in other countries. We can accept this as long as the foreigners who come here are of high quality, help to expand economic activity and thereby help to create job opportunities for Singaporeans — and Singaporeans are always treated fairly.

If we can make this compact work, with all the opportunities coming our way, Singapore has a bright future as an innovative, digital and green economy, at the heart of a dynamic Southeast Asia, creating good jobs and meaningful careers for us all.

Innovation will be the key to our future prosperity. But it must be an inclusive prosperity. I look forward to sharing with you in my next lecture how we can promote a more inclusive society.

Notes

1. Monetary Authority of Singapore estimates; Ministry of Trade and Industry statistics.
2. MAS estimates; Ministry of Manpower statistics.
3. Ibid.
4. MAS estimates; Ministry of Trade and Industry and Ministry of Manpower statistics.
5. Ibid.
6. MAS, "Remarks by Mr Ravi Menon, Managing Director, MAS, at the MAS Annual Report 2019/2020 Virtual Media Conference," July 16, 2020, https://www.mas.gov.sg/news/speeches/2020/remarks-by-mr-ravi-menon-at-the-mas-annual-report-2019-2020-media-conference#5.
7. Singapore Department of Statistics, "Resident Labour Force," [2010–2020 data], accessed July 12, 2021, https://stats.mom.gov.sg/Pages/Labour-Force-Summary-Table.aspx.
8. Singapore Department of Statistics, "Singapore Supply, Use and Input–Output Tables," [2010 and 2017 data], accessed July 12, 2021, https://www.singstat.gov.sg/find-data/search-by-theme/economy/national-accounts/latest-data#SU-IOT; MAS estimates.
9. Paul De Grauwe, *The Limits of the Market*, trans. Anna Asbury (Oxford and New York: Oxford University Press, 2017).

10. Kim Zetter, "Senate Panel: 80 Percent of Cyber Attacks Preventable," *Wired*, November 17, 2009, https://www.wired.com/2009/11/cyber-attacks-preventable.

11. ILO, *World Employment and Social Outlook 2018: Greening With Jobs* (Geneva: International Labour Office, 2018), 1.

12. OECD, "Issue Paper: The Distributional Aspects of Environmental Quality and Environmental Policies: Opportunities for Individuals and Households," November 2018, https://www.oecd.org/greengrowth/GGSD_2018_Households_WEB.pdf, 13.

13. UNEP, *Towards A Green Economy: Pathways to Sustainable Development and Poverty Eradication* (Paris: United Nations Environment Programme, 2011), 1.

14. Leah Lazer, "How Can We Ensure a Just Transition to the Green Economy?" *World Economic Forum*, April 14, 2021, https://www.weforum.org/agenda/2021/04/how-can-we-ensure-a-just-transition-to-the-green-economy.

15. MAS, "Sustainability Report 2020/2021: Managing Director's Foreword," June 9, 2021, https://www.mas.gov.sg/publications/sustainability-report/2021/sustainability-report/foreword.

16. IMF, *Fiscal Monitor: How to Mitigate Climate Change* (Washington, DC: International Monetary Fund, 2009), 7–9; Carbon Pricing Leadership Coalition, "Report of the High-Level Commission on Carbon Prices," May 29, 2017, https://static1.squarespace.com/static/54ff9c5ce4b0a53decccfb4c/t/59b7f2409f8dce5316811916/1505227332748/CarbonPricing_FullReport.pdf, 3.

17. World Bank Group, *States and Trends of Carbon Pricing 2019* (Washington, DC: The World Bank, 2019), 10.

18. Gilbert E. Metcalf and James Stock, "Measuring the Macroeconomic Impact of Carbon Taxes," *AEA Papers and Proceedings* 110 (May 2020).

19. Ministry of Finance, Sweden, "Sweden's Carbon Tax," accessed July 12, 2021, https://www.government.se/government-policy/taxes-and-tariffs/swedens-carbon-tax.

20. Ibid; Swedish Environmental Protection Agency, "Territorial Emissions and Uptake of Greenhouse Gases," accessed July 12, 2021, https://www.naturvardsverket.se/klimatutslapp.

21. WEF, *The Global Competitiveness Report 2019* (Geneva: World Economic Forum, 2019), xiii.

22. Jing Cao, Mun Ho, and Govinda R. Timilsina, "Impacts of Carbon Pricing in Reducing the Carbon Intensity of China's GDP," *World Bank Policy Research Working Paper* 7735 (June 2016).

23. REACH, "Media Release: Majority of Singaporeans Do Not Feel Strongly Negative About Foreigners in Singapore," October 10, 2020, https://www.sgpc. gov.sg/sgpcmedia/media_releases/reach/press_release/ P-20201010-1/attachment/MAJORITY%20OF%20SINGAPOREANS%20DO% 20NOT%20FEEL%20STRONGLY%20NEGATIVE%20ABOUT%20FOREIGNERS% 20IN%20SINGAPORE.pdf.

24. Ibid.

Question-and-Answer Session
Moderated by Mr Chng Kai Fong

Mr Ravi Menon speaking with Mr Chng Kai Fong at his Q&A session
Source: Jacky Ho for the Institute of Policy Studies

Chng Kai Fong: I wanted to connect this to your first lecture. In your first Q&A session, one sentence that you said near the end struck me. You said, or Aristotle said, that democracy survives on the basis of support from the middle. And in that sense, that is the underlying theme running throughout, because what we're trying to do is to insulate and make Singapore thrive as the four horsemen march across Singapore, and one of the key opportunities is to transform ourselves into an innovative economy.

So, I thought, to augment or complement what you have said just now, we can shift our perspectives to just three groups of people that would need to thrive in this new economy, and that would need to transform themselves to be innovative. Let me start with the first group of people, which I would call "the broad middle". These are people in the middle, in their mid-40s to their late 50s, in the midst of transition. They are, in a sense, under pressure from the economic changes. What would you say to these people? Especially as you have sketched out all the drivers of innovation. And you know, you tend to associate innovation with people who are moving in the fast lane — the young and global elite out there in the tech firms. However, the mid-40s and 50s are facing a lot of pressure — they may not have the necessary skills they would need to change jobs. So, how would we help them to thrive in this innovative economy?

Ravi Menon: I'm glad you focused on the middle because I think that's where we should put our minds to, and to make sure that wages and living standards in the broad middle continue to rise. To do that, we need productivity growth.

For productivity growth, I focused on innovation rather than technology. The two tend to get conflated. Technology is about robotics, blockchains, AI and so on. Only about 5 to 10 per cent of the population is going to get into depth on these things; most of us will not have the higher-order cognitive skills for it.

The innovation we want to see — pervasive across the economy and the workforce — is how these technologies are used to change our work processes, to serve our customers better, to reach out to new markets. You see it in financial services for example. The people who write the apps and develop the programmes are a small group of talented engineers. However, we need to be able to use this technology to service our clients better. That requires comfort with technology and an understanding of how to extract the benefits of technology to serve the customer. We are making efforts in this direction. It's too early to tell how far it will succeed. There are some promising examples. For instance, how bank tellers have become financial advisors and digital ambassadors. Has it been pervasive? I would say, not yet. We have got to keep working at this.

The challenge of raising productivity in the middle is something that almost all the major advanced economies face. In their case, it's more difficult because many of the workers in the middle are in the traditional manufacturing sector where activities are hollowing out. I think we can have a better stab at it because we're a smaller country and our workers are more nimble. They have been able to reinvent themselves in the past amid dramatic changes in the structure of the economy. This is not the first time this is happening, right? I remember when I started work in 1987, Singapore's biggest export was disk drives. We were the world's largest producer of Winchester hard drives. Seagate and other companies were producing disk drives here, with large numbers of Singaporeans employed. Today, I don't think we produce any of it. An entire industry has completely offshored. How did we manage the transition? Our manufacturing workforce re-trained and moved on to new activities.

Innovation in the workforce is about the ability to move to adjacent areas, having the enterprising spirit to try something that's not too far out but not entirely within our comfort zone either. If we can do that, we will be in a good place. And that's where most of our reskilling efforts are focused on. But it's not easy, and it doesn't work for everyone because we're all differently equipped.

Mr Chng: What are the challenges that you see today for this particular group of people in trying to move to adjacent areas?

Mr Menon: I'll touch on some of this in my next lecture, on how we need a more flexible labour force. We are currently not very mobile. We are not mobile in respect to changing jobs, we are not mobile in respect to going for overseas postings. We seem to have a lot of encumbrances on our labour flexibility: the need to service mortgages, children's education, and so on. Many households have borrowed to the hilt, and so making career switches that may involve starting with a lower pay becomes more difficult. If you look at successful small European countries like Denmark, they don't have that much baggage. Their workers can uproot, go for training for six months with no pay or with a small stipend, and then move to another job. We can't seem to be able to afford to make such transitions. We need to change that.

There is a role for the government to ease such job transitions. I'm not advocating unemployment benefits, but I think, while a person is training and moving to a new line of work, there ought to be some support. He might be used to a certain lifestyle, he's got a family to feed and financial obligations to meet that cannot be compromised. If we can solve that problem, I think it will make it easier for people to take the leap to do something new. People need to be able to move across jobs, seize new opportunities and learn new things. We need to remove the impediments that somehow seem to have gotten entrenched in Singapore.

Mr Chng: Yeah, just to round that out and flip on the other side: Why should people in this age group have some optimism that this is indeed possible?

Mr Menon: Because of all the opportunities coming our way. Compared with so many of the advanced industrial economies — in America, Europe, Japan — where growth rates have slowed considerably, where median wages have stagnated for 20 years or so, where the nature of growth is so skewed towards the upper end, Singapore is in a much better position. One of the things I've been trying to get across in the lecture, notwithstanding the challenges posed by the four horsemen, which are large, is the range of economic opportunities coming our way, the interest that investors are having in Singapore. People want to come here, people want to do business with us, people want to connect with us. Our trust premium has grown, and our value proposition has grown. So, I don't think there'll be a shortage of new activities. The big question is: Can we seize more of these jobs for Singaporeans? Or whether we have to continue to depend on a growing pool of foreigners to take these jobs? I think there is basis for optimism, but it can be realised only if there is a resolve to step forward to seize the opportunities.

Mr Chng: And now I want to move on to the second category of people, which is our young. And in particular, not just the graduates from our universities but also our polytechnic and ITE graduates. What are some of the challenges we see for this group, in participating in an innovative economy?

Mr Menon: Our polytechnics are world class. There are very few countries that have the equivalent of our polytechnics. The quality of education they receive, which is just short of an academic degree, actually imbibes good strong skills. I think the pity is that their skills are not being utilised well in the economy. One problem we need to resolve is the wage gap. The starting salary gap between a diploma holder and a university graduate is too large, not justified by the difference in skills level. And yet there's something in our labour market that creates this large wedge. Many of our polytechnic students have good skills, but when they can't get a good wage for these skills, they opt to go for degree programmes in softer skills. This is sad because if they hold on to these skills, especially IT and digital, they could be much more valuable and impactful in the digital economy that's emerging.

The bulk of our workforce will have polytechnic education. If we can harness these skills, we'll be in a better place. But I am quite bewildered by the nature of a job market that doesn't give these skills sufficient recognition. That is why continued emphasis on skills rather than education qualifications is important. It is not a cliché, not a slogan, but a real imperative. Employers need to become more enlightened about assessing the skills level of a job seeker rather than take the easy way out of just looking at academic qualifications. I think if we can do that, we can compress some of the wage premiums and make for a more equitable distribution of incomes between the middle and upper middle.

Mr Chng: Yes, and what we've been trying to do is also to integrate some of the education into the workforce. For example, the Singapore Institute of Technology (SIT) and our polytechnics are now doing a lot more internships to bring work experience in.

Mr Menon: Yes, the polytechnics are much more open to collaborating with the industry. They're asking, "Show me your job description, what are the skill sets you're looking out for? I am willing to align my programme and my curriculum to meet that." The more we do that, the link between education and skills training at the job becomes more continuous. This is something all our economic agencies should focus on: To secure as many jobs as possible for our polytechnic students while they are still studying.

Mr Chng: If I were a young person and you were to give me advice, based on the landscape of opportunities you sketched out, what would you advise me to do to thrive in this innovative economy?

Mr Menon: Join a start-up. Not for life; not all of us are cut out to be entrepreneurs. But join a start-up because you will learn first-hand what it takes to build a business and enterprise from scratch. You will have the exhilaration of creating something new — there is no structure, there is no bureaucracy. It is wonderful training. It would be good if we can make as many young Singaporeans, before they start formal work in banks or MNCs, spend two or three years in a start-up. Build character, learn what failure looks like, learn what doors slammed in your face feel like, tinker with technology, learn from other like-minded people, get inspired, and then go on to more stable jobs if that's what you prefer. I've not done it myself but seeing others who have done it, I sometimes feel envious.

Mr Chng: It gives you perspective for sure. Having interacted with people who have been part of university overseas college programmes, polytechnics who send their students to ASEAN start-ups, you can tell that the whole experience changes them. The final group of people that I thought to have you comment on will be our Singapore enterprises, not just SMEs but also the larger firms. What can they do to thrive in an innovative economy? I think we've done a pretty good job over the last 50 odd years. But there are some signs that some of our firms have not quite kept pace with the rest of the global economy. And it doesn't help that, as you said, the bigger tech firms are now exercising monopolistic powers. For the next generation of unicorns and start-ups as you said, what do we have to do differently?

Mr Menon: If you look at the SME sector, there are about 180,000 or close to 200,000 of them, my view is that we need to see consolidation. Given the small size of our domestic economy, it's hard to sustain so many SMEs. Many can't achieve the scale that's required to digitalise, to upgrade, invest in new technology and new capabilities, and to find good people. There is a shortage of good managerial capabilities in many of our SMEs. There are financial incentives to make mergers more attractive, but many SME owners value their independence though they are running their businesses in a rather unproductive way and they are not able to give good wages to their workers. It's a problem we haven't solved.

Second, I'm excited by the emerging possibilities for digital connectivity because that surmounts a big problem that our smaller enterprises face. Few of them have the resources to go out to the region, make a trip to Indonesia, go and meet clients, rent a place and do all the logistics necessary to set up businesses and supply chains, and effectively serve an external market from out of Singapore. Digital platforms democratise and open up access. If you're able to get onto these platforms, you can find suppliers, customers, financiers, partners, logistics providers, and so on, much more effectively. As these platforms get better, say using AI and data analytics, the information flow would become richer. The world becomes the SME's oyster. I hope we can get more of our SMEs onto platforms such as the NTP, BSB and all the other acronyms that I mentioned.

Mr Chng: Hopefully that gives a boost. I want to compare ourselves with let's say the Swiss economy. In EDB, we see many multinationals and we always hold ourselves to the benchmarks of the Swiss — ABB, Roche, Novartis, Nestlé — massively huge players that have gone out and become global names. We are almost similar in terms of population size, our education is not too bad either, and we are also digitally connected. How is it that we are not able to match up to what the Swiss have achieved?

Mr Menon: I too admire Switzerland, having lived there for a year. What I am about to say is not deeply insightful, and mostly impressionistic. The Swiss place a great deal of value on learning, inventiveness and excellence. Their pharmaceutical industry is world class, and they also make the best chocolates, wonderful watches and excellent food products. There is pride in work. There is a culture of craftsmanship built over generations — taking pride in what you produce, making it the best in class for your customer. Whether it's making a drug, watch or fine chocolate, you see that excellence.

Swiss society is also a lot more egalitarian. They don't have large differences in incomes, because I guess the dignity of all work is strong. Everyone has a commitment to excellence. Someone is quite happy to be making chocolates because he is making some of the best chocolates in the world. There is no mad rush for everyone to get into white-collar jobs in big banks. Of course, the Swiss banks are also world class, but they're not very large like J.P. Morgan or Goldman Sachs. Many are small banks, providing highly specialised services. Even if you look at private banking, aside from UBS and Credit Suisse, the Swiss private banking industry is mostly small boutique banks providing very customised, highly specialised services. So, there's something about their culture that is customer-focused, excellence-focused, wanting to learn continuously and being flexible. These are not alien to us. We have some of these qualities in our own DNA. But there are other forces at work here that kind of constrain us, and if we can free ourselves of those, we too can become like the Swiss.

Mr Chng: Yeah, I think we certainly can if we have the will to do that. So, I'm going to take some audience questions right now. Maybe let's start with a question on distortions in the labour market: What are the distortions in our labour market and how can we fix them, especially in the non-tradable segments? Do we have wage repression in favour of returns to real estate owners? Are workers in the wrong profession? We have many great delivery drivers and riders, insurance and real estate salespeople, but a shortage of nurses and construction workers. What should we be doing differently?

Mr Menon: It's a good and troubling question. I too have often wondered about the wage differentials across different occupations. I am going to touch on this in my third lecture. For instance, why are plumbers paid relatively less in Singapore than in advanced countries? Why are our electricians paid so much less? Somebody who repairs your car, a whole lot of skilled professions. If I have a leak in the house, I need the plumber. But why is his pay so much lower? Across quite a number of these kinds of jobs, the pay is low: nurses, teachers of special needs children, childcare specialists, and so on. Many of these people facing jobs do not require a high degree of academic brilliance, but they do require lots of EQ and quite specific skill sets. So, when we speak about income inequality, it's much more important to look at occupational wage inequality and examine why occupations are paid so differently. What is it in our market that brings this about? I think if we can understand that, we can better address our concerns about income inequality. So, I agree with the import of the question — there seems to be some problem in our labour market, in the way reward structures are determined.

One of the reasons why I think the wages of some of these jobs is low is because we have a large foreign workforce in these occupations. As these foreign workers come cheap, it keeps the cost of many of these services low. We have accepted the lower wages in these jobs. This is the dual economy trap that we need to escape from, which is why I was making the case that we should gradually reduce our dependence on foreign labour for many of these skilled jobs in the middle. I'm not talking about the top end. For many of these skilled jobs, like nurses and so on, over time, we must allow the wages to rise to a point where it's attractive for Singaporeans to come into these jobs. That I think will raise the status of these jobs and make the middle much stronger. The catch is that costs will go up — from hawker centre food to healthcare costs, plumbing services, house repairs, renovation — because we're getting skilled Singaporeans to do these jobs. We have to deal with that. Our big challenge is to escape this low-cost, low-wage vicious cycle, and instead get into a high-cost, high-wage paradigm. The high costs are affordable for most people because most people have high wages. Again, think Switzerland.

Mr Chng: The question is, how do we get there? What's the journey to get there, and what are the transition costs?

Mr Menon: The transition costs will not be small. We would have to gradually reduce the dependence on foreign labour. Costs will rise, some of these firms will have to consolidate and there may have to be some kind of fiscal support for the workers who are stranded and need to transit to new jobs. I mentioned the example of the Ruhr valley, where 480,000 coal miners lost their jobs but transited into new jobs. How did they do that? Well, it's over time, it's careful planning, it's the kind of stuff Singapore is good at. If the Germans can do it, we can do it too. However, we need the will to do it and the ability to bear some of the adjustment costs. We have taken, in my view, the easy way out, in a desire to always keep costs low. I think we are overly obsessed with cost competitiveness, not realising that keeping costs low is actually keeping wages down.

Mr Chng: We've got a related question but this time more on the higher end on the Comprehensive Economic Cooperation Agreement (CECA) and immigration. The question is this: As much as it's true that Singapore is in an excellent position to leverage a cosmopolitan society with an international outlook, we cannot ignore the fact that many Singaporeans feel threatened with the inflow of talent from a particular nationality.

Irrespective of whether it's real or perceived, it needs to be addressed. How do you think we can continue to seek growth without the risk of fracturing our already fragile social fabric? I imagine you'd be touching on some of that in the third lecture, but perhaps you could focus more on the seeking growth part without causing more fractures.

Mr Menon: We should focus the national discourse on the complementarity between local and foreign workers. In a limited MAS study on financial services, we found that at the higher end, local and foreign workers are complementary. So we are quite confident that at the higher end, Singaporeans are not losing jobs to foreigners. Of course, there will always be exceptions and there will be some substitution, but by and large it's been complementary. We need to examine this more closely across the economy, and to see and satisfy ourselves, if the complementary relationship indeed holds between locals and foreigners in all industries. I'm not sure of that entirely because I don't think we've studied that data carefully. But this is something we need to do. And if we do find that there are some areas where the substitution effects are stronger, where foreigners are actually taking the jobs that Singaporeans could have done, then we have to rethink our policies in those areas. My own view is that, by and large, the relationship is complementary.

Most Singaporeans, according to polls, agree that the foreign workforce creates opportunity here and thereby helps create jobs for Singaporeans. But if you are that unlucky person who lost your job, it's still painful. Where the lived reality is different from the statistical fact, we have to address that lived reality as well. That's why I think we need to take this at two points. One is to demonstrate the complementarity so that, at least intellectually, people understand that the intake of foreign talent is good for us. Then there is also the emotional part, where we need to help those who have lost their jobs. We need to get them transitioned into new jobs, which we discussed earlier on. It is not easy but there is a variety of initiatives, conversion programmes, and so on, to give them a leg up. We may need to change some of our active labour market policies to support our displaced to move on to new jobs. I think if we can do these things, we can maintain a reasonable social compact on staying open. It's not going to be easy but I think we can do better than what we are at risk of slipping into right now.

Mr Chng: I have another question on the ageing population and on women. With an ageing population, the labour force declines because we're not being innovative enough with how we maximise the capabilities of two groups of people. One, older people, and two, women with care responsibilities. These two groups of people create opportunities for the creation of new jobs and services so that they're not a drag on the economy. What do you think are the opportunities for these two groups of people?

Mr Menon: The government has been making efforts to keep older workers longer in the workforce. To some extent I think it has worked because our labour force participation rate for seniors has improved. At least, it's not bad by international comparisons, so we're not doing too badly. To be realistic, I think further increases in participation rate are going to be difficult. We have to understand the economics facing many firms. They need fresh young talents who can master new technologies and new ways of working. It may well be that the gig economy shifts from the younger group to the older group. In fact, I think it is a pity that too many young people are in the gig economy, because these are years when they should be having solid jobs — whether it's at a start-up, multinational or a local enterprise — building skills, building capabilities, and not take the easy way of quick bucks that you can get in a gig economy. But for the older workers, gig work is a real possibility.

Likewise, for women who have childbearing responsibilities and find it difficult to hold on to a full-time job, gig economy type services that you can provide from the home, through a computer, through a digital platform, are possibilities. Older workers as well as women who are not able to join the formal workforce could explore these options. Retirement adequacy is an issue for some: people are living longer, and even if they work to 65 or 67, they still have many years left. They may have to look at possibilities in gig work. It will be interesting if entrepreneurs and social enterprises come up with ideas on how to tap on the talents of older workers.

Mr Chng: In fact, we tend to associate start-ups with 20 somethings, 30 somethings, but actually we could flip it around. Well, one last question and the obligatory question on education, which always pops up in every one of these lectures: In striving towards a frontier economy that prizes innovation, is the existing school curriculum sufficient? Should there be more emphasis on personal development and creativity? But let me extend that. What do we need to do to improve our education system, not just for pre-employment but also throughout life? What are some of the necessary capabilities or skills that we need to equip our people with?

Mr Menon: Well, I just said we have a very good education system and I mean it: we do. Our system produces high-quality workers — a good range of skills and the right attitudes. But in terms of creativity and innovation, it is a bit different. The common perception, which I think has quite a bit of truth to, is that this is not an area Singaporeans are particularly strong at. I think our education system needs to focus more on exploring questions rather than finding answers. Creativity and innovation are about asking the right questions. The "what if" kinds of questions are not often emphasised. There is much rush to cover a lot of content, which of course is necessary, but because we also need to then decide who goes where, we have many tests. That in turn means we focus on finding the answers to those questions that come out in the test.

Mr Chng: So we assume there's a right answer.

Mr Menon: Yes, generations of Singaporeans have come through the education system with the notion that there is a right answer. When we go to work, we're again looking for the right answer. But actually, we should be spending time on asking the right questions. That's what opens up new avenues and insights. We see this everywhere in our work: we are always trying to find the right answer but never stopping to ask what is the right question. This rush to find answers, I think, stifles creativity. We need to be able to handle uncertainty and understand that sometimes questions can have multiple answers. As F. Scott Fitzgerald said, "The mark of intelligence is the ability to hold two contradictory ideas in your mind at the same time." It will also make us less fixated on our own views and help us be more broad-minded, which is another ingredient for creativity and innovation.

Mr Chng: And on that note, I thought that's a good way to end, given that your lecture has probably raised many more questions than answers. Hopefully that will be the spirit that carries us going forward. Thank you, Ravi.

Lecture III
AN INCLUSIVE SOCIETY

Social inclusion is close to the hearts of many people in Singapore. I have received many comments and questions following my first two lectures — almost all were on the issues of inequality and inclusion. Earlier, I asked a few people for ideas for this lecture on an inclusive society. All of them replied with long emails; one Singaporean lady whom I have not even met before sent me a 14-page letter. I am thankful and overwhelmed — by their feedback and ideas, but more importantly that they care deeply to make Singapore a more inclusive society.

Inequality and inclusion are related but distinct. A perfectly equal society is neither feasible nor desirable. Inequality of outcomes reflects inequality of ability and effort, and luck. An equal society will not be seen as just or fair by most people.

I believe what most of us want instinctively is an inclusive society — one that provides broadly equal opportunity for all to move up in life; one that leaves no one behind; one that treats all with dignity and respect; in short, one that makes everyone feel included. Or as Martin Sandbu from the *Financial Times* puts it: to create "an economy of belonging", where the markets work for everyone.[1] Of course, a highly unequal society is unlikely to be inclusive. But rather than try to make society more equal, it might be better to focus on the tangible elements that make it more inclusive.

In my first lecture, I said inequality becomes socially unacceptable and economically inefficient when it leads to *increased poverty, middle class stagnation,* a *growing wealth gap* or *reduced social mobility.*

So, let me start the lecture with a quick overview of how Singapore fares on these four primarily economic dimensions of inclusion: low-wage workers, median wage growth, wealth gap and social mobility. I fully recognise that there are many other aspects of social inclusion but I will focus on these four. But first let me briefly deal with the ubiquitous Gini coefficient and get it out of the way.

Much Ado About the Gini

There is much ado about the Gini coefficient, but it is really not the best lens to view the issue of social inclusion. To recap, the Gini coefficient measures the extent to which the Lorenz curve (which plots the percentage of income earned by x per cent of the population) deviates from a 45-degree line. A Gini coefficient of zero implies perfect equality and one implies perfect inequality.

Singapore's Gini coefficient after taxes and transfers is 0.34. It is higher than many European countries, especially the Nordic countries that are at around 0.27, as well as Canada at 0.30, comparable to Australia at 0.33, but lower than the United Kingdom at 0.37 and the United States at 0.39.[2] Cities tend to have higher Gini coefficients; and we are a global city at that. City-level Gini coefficients are hard to come by on a comparable basis. But for what it is worth, Hong Kong had a much higher Gini coefficient of 0.47 in 2016. But unlike Hong Kong, Singapore is also a country. A country cannot afford to have such high inequality.

But the Gini coefficient is highly sensitive to observations in the extreme upper and lower ends of the income distribution. A small number of extremely high-income earners can significantly affect the Gini coefficient without any change in the rest of the distribution. For example, if there are 10 of us in a room with varying income levels, we can compute a Gini coefficient to measure the degree of income inequality among us. But if Roger Federer or Cristiano Ronaldo walked into the room, the Gini coefficient would immediately rise, indicating greater inequality. Yet nothing has changed among the original 10 of us in the room.

Interdecile income ratios are likely to give us a more meaningful perspective of income distribution. For example, looking at the ratio of the income of those between the 80th and 90th percentiles to those between zero and 10th percentiles gets rid of the outlier effects and yet tells us how the top incomes and bottom incomes are faring relative to one another. In 2000, the average monthly household income from work per household member at the 90th percentile was 18 times that of the household at the 10th percentile; that ratio went up to 26 times over 2008 to 2012 before easing slightly to around 24 times in more recent years. But if we look at the ratio of the household income per member at the 80th percentile to that of the 10th percentile, we see a gentler increase: from about nine times in 2000 to about 11 times in 2005 and staying fairly stable at around that level till now (Figure 1).

So, income inequality has obviously worsened in both the decile comparisons. But what is interesting is that while the gap between the 90th percentile and the 10th percentile has widened considerably over the last 20 years, the gap between the 80th percentile and 10th percentile household has increased only slightly and has been roughly stable for the last 15 years — which is quite remarkable. This underscores what I said earlier about the "Roger Federer effect" — the sharp increases in income at the top make the measured income inequality worse than is the case for the majority of the population. The Gini coefficient tracks the P90/P10 ratio more closely. It shows a marked worsening over the 2000s and a slight improvement from about 2012 onwards (Figure 1).

Figure 1.   Ratio of Household Income from Work at the 90th and 80th Percentiles to the 10th Percentile and Gini Coefficient*

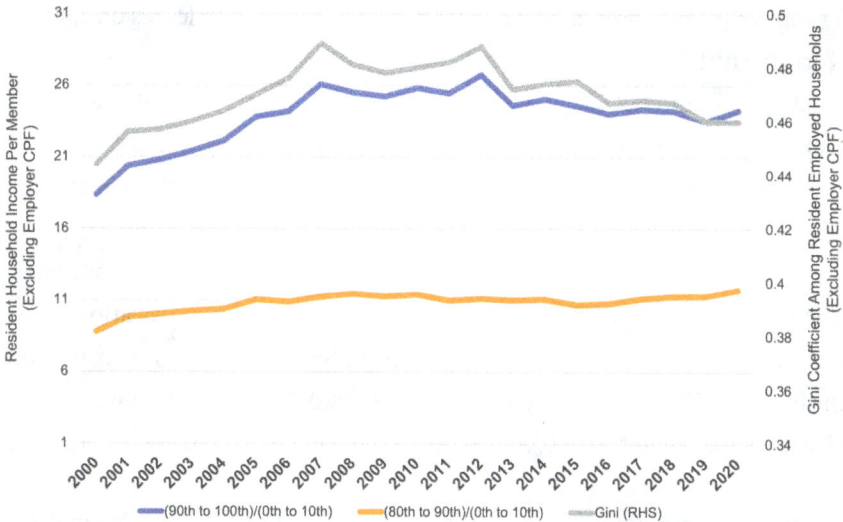

*Average monthly household income from work per household member (excluding employer CPF contributions) among resident employed households.

Source: Singapore Department of Statistics, "Average Monthly Household Income from Work Per Household Member (Excluding Employer CPF Contributions) Among Resident Employed Households by Deciles," [2000–2020 data], accessed July 20, 2021, https://tablebuilder.singstat.gov.sg/table/CT/17251; Singapore Department of Statistics, "Gini Coefficient Among Resident Employed Households (Excluding Employer CPF Contributions)," [2000–2020 data], accessed July 20, 2021, https://tablebuilder.singstat.gov.sg/table/CT/17206.

The Anatomy of an Inclusive Economy

Let me come back to how Singapore fares on the four aspects of an inclusive economy: little poverty, decent median wage growth, a stable wealth gap and social mobility.

Low-Wage Workers

There is very little absolute poverty in Singapore, so it makes more sense to focus on low-wage workers. We could look at the wage gap between those at the 20th percentile (P20) of the income distribution and the median (P50). In 2001, the wage of the worker at the 20th percentile was 58 per cent of the median wage. This P20/P50 ratio deteriorated over the following 10 years to reach a low of 50 per cent in 2012. With the government deploying a range of policy tools, such as tighter quotas and higher levies on foreign work permit holders, the P20/P50 ratio has improved in recent years, reaching 54 per cent in 2019 before dipping to 52 per cent last year as the COVID-19 recession hit lower-income workers harder. But even at the recent peak of 54 per cent, we are still below the level 20 years ago (Figure 2).

Singapore's P20/P50 ratio looks low compared to OECD countries. The OECD convention is to publish the P10/P50 ratio. This ratio ranges from 50 per cent in the US to 74 per cent in Sweden, with most countries in the 60 to 70 per cent range.[3] Singapore's P20/P50 ratio at 52 per cent is already lower than the P10/P50 ratio in many OECD countries. Countries

Figure 2. Ratio of Household Income from Work at the 20th to the 50th Percentiles**

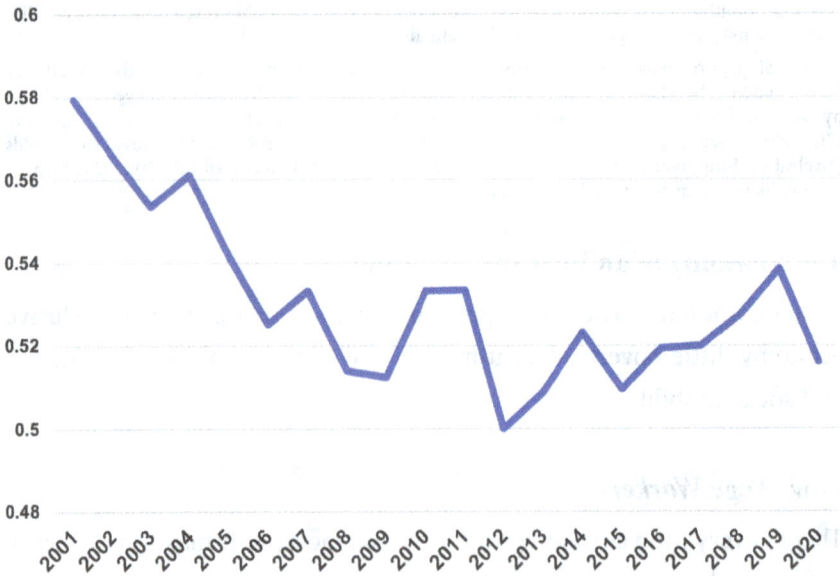

**Average monthly household income from work per household member (excluding employer CPF contributions) among resident employed households.

Source: Ministry of Manpower, "Report: Labour Force in Singapore: 2020 Edition," January 28, 2021, https:// stats.mom.gov.sg/iMAS_PdfLibrary/mrsd_2020LabourfForce.pdf, 38.

such as the UK, US, and South Korea have national minimum wages and others such as Norway and Sweden have strong industry-led minimum wage regulations.

Median Wage Growth

Singapore's experience with median wages has not been bad. As I mentioned in my first lecture, real median wages increased by an average of 2.6 per cent per annum from 2011 to 2020, higher than the 1.2 per cent annual growth from 2001 to 2010.[4]

The stronger real median wage growth from 2011 to 2020 was underpinned by good gross domestic product (GDP) growth. Growth was relatively broad-based across sectors from 2011 to 2015, followed by strong growth in labour productivity from 2016 to 2020. The tightening of foreign worker policies through the decade led to a strong demand for resident labour, particularly in domestic-oriented services sectors. The transition from labour-intensive production to higher value-added activities in manufacturing, coupled with strong growth in high-paying services sectors such as finance, insurance and information and communications technology (ICT) also helped support healthy median wage growth. Falling inflation rates from 2013 onwards boosted wage growth in real terms.

Wealth Gap

Statistics from almost all nations that measure wealth in their household surveys indicate that it is becoming increasingly concentrated.[5] The widening wealth gap has historically been driven most strongly by property investments.[6] People with higher incomes can afford larger investments in real estate and the substantial value appreciation they enjoy over time is not available to those with lower incomes and smaller outlays for housing.

Singapore does not have good data on wealth but it would appear that to some extent, this property-induced increase in wealth inequality is also occurring here. The higher income groups are likely to have grown their wealth proportionately faster than the lower income groups, given the boom in the private residential market and multiple property purchases by the rich.

However, Singapore's heavy subsidisation of public housing and high rate of home ownership would have mitigated some of the divergence in housing wealth. In very few countries do most citizens have the opportunity to enjoy capital appreciation in housing assets as we do in Singapore. But if price increases in private housing consistently outstrip that in public housing, wealth inequality will worsen over time, even if not to the same extent as in many other countries.

To promote an inclusive society, it might make sense to shift the balance in our tax structure away from taxing income towards taxing wealth. Singapore's wealth taxation has indeed become more significant and progressive over the last 10 years. There is probably room to go further in that direction. A wealth tax could take the form of either a property gains tax or an inheritance tax.

But taxing wealth has not worked well in many countries. In 1990, 12 European countries levied an annual tax on net wealth. By 2018, eight out of the 12 countries had abandoned the wealth tax, citing high administrative costs, risk of capital flight and ironically, failure to meet redistributive goals.[7] This is not necessarily a reason for not imposing a wealth tax, but a strong caution that designing a good wealth tax is not a trivial exercise.

Social Mobility

Income mobility — the ability to change one's economic status — is a crucial component of an inclusive society.

Singapore is not doing too badly in terms of income mobility across generations. According to a 2015 study by the Ministry of Finance, the percentage of young Singaporeans (in their 30s) — with parents in the lowest income quintile when they were growing up — who have moved up to the top quintile of income earners as adults was 14 per cent. This is higher

**Figure 3.   Proportion of Children Born to Parents in the Bottom Income Quintile
Reaching the Top Income Quintile**

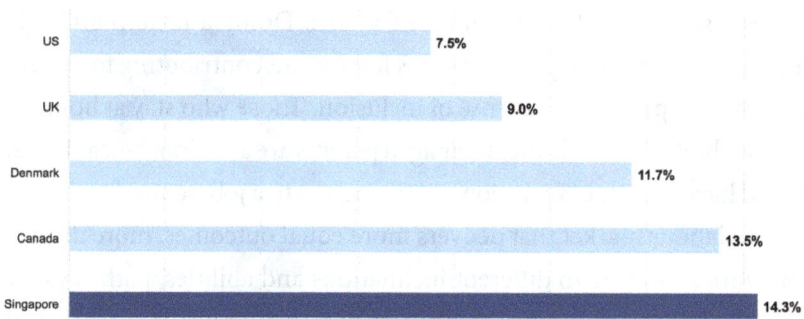

Source: Ministry of Finance, "(2015) Income Growth, Inequality and Mobility Trends in Singapore,"
August 2015, https://www.mof.gov.sg/docs/default-source/default-document-library/news-and-
publications/featured-reports/income-growth-distribution-and-mobility-trends-in-singapore.pdf, 19.

than even countries such as Canada and Denmark, which have more
equitable income distributions (Figure 3).

But it is going to get more difficult over time to sustain mobility. Our
positive intergenerational income mobility situation essentially reflects
earlier waves of mobility. The 1980s and 1990s, when these cohorts grew
up, were a period of rapid economic growth, accompanied by a significant
expansion in education and job opportunities. Singaporeans who came of
age during this period enjoyed opportunities that their parents did not; and
so they did better. The degree of mobility in society today will only be
discernible later.

The key is to maintain as level a playing field as possible for younger
Singaporeans, especially early in life. Of some concern is that, despite efforts,
the proportion of children from lower-income households enrolling in
preschool is much lower than for higher income households. Given how
keen competition is in Singapore and how hard parents in higher income
households work to give their children a head start, as a society we must
be relentless in making sure that children from less advantaged families
have every opportunity to build up their capabilities and confidence, to do
well in school and subsequently in life.

A Jobs and Wage Architecture for Inclusion

Singapore's social inclusion agenda must be centred on jobs and wages. A job gives a sense of fulfilment and self-worth. Doing a meaningful job, earning a decent wage, supporting one's family and contributing to society are critically important for a sense of inclusion. Those who stay at home to raise their children or look after their aged parents are also doing meaningful work and have a sense of inclusion. Fundamental to a job-centred inclusion model is a labour market that delivers more equal outcomes, more diverse opportunities catering to different inclinations and abilities, pathways for those at the bottom of the income distribution to upgrade themselves and springboards to help those who fall to bounce back. Redistribution through taxes and transfers also has an important role in fostering inclusion, but it is secondary to a labour market-centred model of inclusion.

A job-centred social inclusion agenda must aim to raise the wages of low-wage workers, sustain median wage growth and promote income mobility. We cannot rely on any single measure to achieve all this; we need to deploy a range of tools. Such a multi-faceted agenda also calls for a creative synthesis of prescriptions from across the ideological spectrum: highly flexible and competitive labour markets, coupled with active labour market policies to share risk and responsibility among workers, employers and the state.

We need a comprehensive architecture to enhance inclusion through jobs and wages: *safety nets* to provide a basic level of support, *trampolines* to help people bounce back if they fall and *escalators* to help people move up along progressively higher wages.

Let us imagine a job and wage architecture that comprises two safety nets, one trampoline and four escalators. The two safety nets are a *minimum wage* and an *enhanced Workfare Income Supplement* (WIS). The trampoline is *re-employment support*. The four escalators are *progressive wages, reclaimed jobs, professionalised jobs* and *lifelong learning*. Most of these tools already exist, and what is new builds on the existing architecture that has served Singaporeans reasonably well so far.

Safety Net I: Minimum Wage

The first safety net, a most basic one: minimum wage. Proponents of a minimum wage argue that it will help uplift low-wage workers and reduce income inequality. Its opponents maintain that it will displace low-wage workers and create more unemployment. I think both the benefits and costs may be overstated and that we might want to seriously study a modest minimum wage. It is not a straightforward issue. I have changed my view of the minimum wage three times over the last 35 years: from no to yes, then to no again and now yes. Let me explain.

There is a large body of empirical evidence across countries that find zero or minimal adverse effects on employment from an increase in the minimum wage. In a recent wide-ranging survey of the empirical literature, British economist Alan Manning describes the employment effect of minimum wages as "elusive" or hard to find.[8] The increase in the wage bill arising from a minimum wage is mostly passed through to higher prices and partly absorbed in profit margins; this varies across sectors and industries. There is no free lunch.

A different way to pose the question might be this: instead of asking whether we should have a minimum wage, why not ask at what level might we set it at? Years ago, I asked an economist from the Asian Development Bank if a minimum wage was a good idea. He said, "It depends on where you set it." So, let us imagine a minimum wage of say S$1,200 per month. The key question then is: What are the likely effects on wages, employment and prices in different industries? What is the wage distribution of workers earning below the S$1,200 level? If most of them are bunched close to S$1,200, there is a good chance the positive wage effect could be sizeable while the negative employment effect is trivial. But if most of these workers are well below S$1,200, there is a chance that many of them may become unemployed. Is there scope to move them to other jobs?

I should add though that the benefits of a minimum wage should not be exaggerated. Some well-meaning proponents of the minimum wage in Singapore view it as a means to reduce income inequality. I do not think that a minimum wage — at the reasonable levels that are being talked about — will make a discernible dent in income inequality. If we have a minimum wage, we must be clear of its rationale: it is to help lift the wages of those at the bottom of the income distribution. A minimum wage also signifies a societal value: that no one should be paid less than this amount for his or her labour. It is not unlike setting minimum standards for workplace safety and humane conditions of work.

For raising the wage prospects of the majority of our low-wage workers, the sector-based Progressive Wage Model (PWM) is more effective than a national minimum wage. Why then have a minimum wage? Well, it is not clear whether the PWM can be extended to all occupations below the 30th percentile, how long it will take and whether it will work as well. The minimum wage and progressive wage need not be alternatives; they could be complements.

If a national minimum wage is seen as too big a step, we could more decisively use the Local Qualifying Salary (LQS) as a de facto minimum wage. Today, the LQS already serves as a de facto minimum wage for Singaporeans in firms that bring in a large number of foreign workers. This is how it works: firms that bring in foreign workers are subject to a Dependency Ratio Ceiling (DRC) that sets a limit on the number of foreign workers they can bring in relative to resident workers. The DRC in the service sector is 35 per cent — in other words, up to 35 per cent of the firm's total workforce can be foreign workers.[9] The LQS is the minimum wage that must be paid to resident workers so that these resident workers can count towards the firm's total workforce for purposes of computing the number of foreign workers the firm can employ within the DRC. Firms must thus pay enough local workers the LQS at least, in order to build up a quota of foreign workers that they can employ, which is capped by the DRC.

We could consider steadily increasing the LQS over time. The LQS is currently S$1,400; for the last few years, it has been going up by S$100 every year.[10] We could continue doing so or even step up the increases.

An increase in the LQS is likely to have positive wage effects for low-wage workers. An internal study by the Monetary Authority of Singapore (MAS) in 2020 found that an increase in the LQS raises the effective minimum wage for resident workers in a good proportion of firms in the services sector, with positive effects on wages among resident workers in the lower half of the wage distribution. An increase in the LQS has some negative effects on employment, but the negative impact is greater on foreign employment than on resident employment.

One drawback of using the LQS as a de facto minimum wage is that firms that are not yet hitting their DRC would not need to pay the marginal resident worker the LQS. But so long as these firms need to hire foreigners at all, they would still have to pay some of their locals the LQS, and it would make sense for them to extend this wage to other locals doing the same job, for the sake of parity.

For any form of minimum wage to work, we would need to simultaneously raise the price of foreigners relative to locals. Although one way to do it would be to raise foreign worker levies, the levy increase could simply be passed down to the foreign worker in terms of wage reductions, leading to a reduction in labour quality.

These are not straightforward issues; they need careful study. My sense is that some kind of wage floor, either through a formal minimum wage or using the LQS as an active proxy, may need to be part of the overall wage architecture for a more inclusive economy.

Safety Net II: Workfare Income Supplement

The second safety net in our jobs and wages architecture is the WIS. Introduced in 2007, WIS tops up the salaries of workers up to the 30th percentile; it is paid in cash to supplement their take-home pay and as top-ups to their Central Provident Fund (CPF) accounts to boost their retirement savings.

The key innovation in WIS is that it provides a framework to increase support for low-wage workers without increasing dependency. It was born out of the conviction that the best way to help low-wage and unemployed workers was not through expanding the welfare system but to make the work system more rewarding — to encourage low-wage workers to stay in work and to encourage the unemployed to seek work. Unlike receiving transfers, being paid higher wages for work maintains one's sense of dignity in the job.

WIS has been a largely successful programme. WIS top-ups can comprise up to an extra 30 per cent of a worker's monthly income. Since 2007, more than 300,000 workers have been receiving WIS benefits each year.[11] Enhancements to the WIS in 2020 are estimated to have benefitted close to 440,000 Singaporeans.[12] A 2014 study by the Ministry of Trade and Industry found that the WIS was effective in incentivising less-educated Singaporeans, particularly in the older age groups, to enter and stay in the workforce.[13]

Trampoline: Re-employment Support

Besides safety nets, we need a trampoline to help workers bounce back from falls — specifically transitional support for re-employment. In my first lecture, I mentioned how the third horseman — technology — was changing the nature of our jobs. Dealing with this successfully requires a more dynamic and flexible labour market characterised by a high degree of job destruction, creation and mobility. Such a dynamic labour market will require more security for workers than we currently have. This means some form of temporary unemployment benefit or insurance to ease the transition of workers from redundant jobs to skills training before they can take on new jobs. Denmark is an oft-cited example of how a minimum level of income security promotes a flexible and dynamic labour market.

We need meaningful labour mobility — which means identifying and training for jobs that suit our abilities and aptitudes rather than taking the first job that comes along. Today, we have a small group of young serial job switchers with poor wage outcomes. We have a larger group of older workers at risk of redundancy as automation becomes more pervasive, and they would need to move to new jobs. But both groups will need time, facilitation and financial resources to re-chart their careers; search for and identify the jobs that match their abilities and aspirations; and acquire the skills and capabilities to do those jobs.

Re-employment support will help minimise underemployment and enhance the skills and adaptability of structurally unemployed workers. It will help them take the risks of transiting to new growth areas. It could also serve as a small automatic stabiliser during economic downturns by supporting domestic consumption.

Without a mechanism to save workers, we are forced to save jobs — and that may not always be a good idea. Rather, we should let jobs that have become obsolete die out and businesses that have become unviable to unwind and focus our efforts on training and moving workers into higher-paying jobs.

We need to foster greater labour market dynamism through more efficient reallocation of workers rather than protect jobs through assistance delivered to employers. Our current approach of supporting workers by subsidising their existing jobs through transfers to firms may have to gradually pivot to directly supporting workers and their retraining into the new jobs of the future. This could be through subsidised attach-and-train schemes with growth firms short of skilled workers. Such schemes are already available today and we should see how they can be scaled up as part of a comprehensive re-employment support programme.

A word of caution: we should design support measures as re-employment facilitation rather than as unemployment benefits. Providing assistance without a deliberate link to employment search and active upskilling leads to poor outcomes, as shown by the experience in many countries. A well-designed re-employment support programme should be time-bound. Prolonged unemployment benefits reduce the motivation to work. Canada and Poland have done it quite smartly. They set the maximum duration of support depending on the business cycle; a longer duration when the unemployment rate is higher and the probability of finding a job is lower.[14]

Escalator I: Progressive Wages

The first escalator is the PWM, which provides a framework for wages to improve as workers become more skilled.

There are some administration and support industries in Singapore where firms have tended to rely on business models that keep labour costs low. With a relatively small number of firms in these industries and foreign workers widely available, employers had some monopsony power over their local workers in setting wages and benefits.[15] It is a clear case where the labour market was imperfect and not working well. Competition was limited, labour mobility was not high and wages were therefore depressed.

The PWM has helped to map training and career pathways for workers to improve their productivity in three such industries — cleaning, landscaping and security services. Levies for foreign work permit holders were increased, which helped to curb the monopsony power of the employers and improve the bargaining position of local workers. These measures have enabled the workers in these sectors to enjoy wage increases in line with improvements in productivity. Higher productivity in turn has improved service quality and business profits.

The PWM has been successful in lifting the wage growth of these sectors. PWM sectors have seen cumulative wage growth of around 30 per cent, compared with 21 per cent for workers at the median.[16] Unlike a static minimum wage, the PWM acts as a wage escalator based on a framework of industry-recognised qualifications and competencies.

The PWM's coverage needs to be broadened. We need a PWM to help workers in other industries facing similar conditions of low levels of wages and low rates of wage growth. Today, the PWM covers only 3 per cent of the resident workforce. The government is committed to extend the PWM to more industries, but it will take time as it involves intensive tripartite consultations.

The way tender processes are carried out for the services covered under the PWM could be relooked. Cleaning companies have complained that contracts continue to be awarded to the cheapest bidders, who often pay their workers the lowest wages. This makes it economically unviable for companies who want to abide by the PWM because they might lose their contracts.[17] Factors such as the local manpower share, technology and productivity parameters could be given higher weightage in tender evaluation. It has been suggested that government take the lead in best-sourcing service contracts and hopefully companies in the private sector would follow suit.[18]

Escalator II: Reclaiming Jobs for Locals

Even with the PWM, firms may have less incentive to hire locals at higher wages and adopt new technology if they still have access to an ample supply of cheap foreign workers.

This brings us to the second escalator: reclaiming jobs for locals.

We need to be more deliberate in reducing the number of foreign workers in domestic non-tradable sectors and freeing up these jobs for Singaporeans. This cannot be done in one step without creating large disruptions. But if we tighten the intake of low-skilled foreign labour in a determined and progressive manner over a few years, it would help drive restructuring in these industries, promote the adoption of technology and increase productivity, and help to sustain wage gains across a wider range of occupations. There are about 620,000 resident workers in so-called "blue-collar" jobs — that is, service and sales workers, craftsmen, operators and labourers, but excluding clerical workers. The median wage of these occupations, including employer CPF, ranges from S$1,500 to S$2,350.[19] Aside from foreign work permit holders in the construction, marine shipyard and process sectors, as well as migrant domestic workers, there are about 290,000 work permit holders in the rest of the economy — a majority of them working in similar blue-collar jobs as the 620,000 resident workers.[20] As a rough estimate, one out of three low-wage service jobs are taken up by cheap foreign labour. This cannot be good for local wages.

The demand for many domestic services such as cleaning, maintenance and cooking is inelastic, and wages will have to go up if the number of foreign workers is reduced. The increase in wages, coupled with improvements in work conditions and prospects for a meaningful career, should gradually attract Singaporeans into these domestic services.

The transition will no doubt be challenging. Firms whose business models rely excessively on low-cost labour will have to exit. There may have to be some consolidation in these industries, such as retail and food and beverage. It is likely that there would be local job losses in the initial phase. Moving from a low-wage equilibrium, such as the one we are in now, to a high-wage equilibrium, such as the one we aspire to, is always a tricky business.

The reclaiming of local jobs should extend beyond low-wage workers to the broad middle as well. I asked in my second lecture whether we should consider gradually raising the minimum qualifying salary for S Pass holders closer to the median wage of S$4,500 from the current S$2,500. S Pass holders would be in mid-tier Associate Professional and Technician (APT) jobs; at S$2,500 today, the minimum qualifying salary for S Pass holders is significantly lower than the median gross income from work of APTs, which is S$4,150 (including employer CPF).[21]

I am not suggesting that S Pass workers should be drastically curtailed. Many of them are making valuable contributions to our economy and society. How could we have coped with COVID-19 last year if we did not have the many nurses here on S Pass? But when S Pass holders are available in such large numbers and paid around 30 per cent less than locals, there are two possible effects. One, local wages are likely being depressed; and two, some of our Institute of Technical Education (ITE) and polytechnic graduates are probably being competed out of these jobs. Why not pay S Pass workers closer to the local median and let the market settle the employment profile? In some occupations, we might see an increase in local employment at better wages; in other occupations, where Singaporeans are unable or unwilling to enter, we will continue to employ S Pass holders.

The scope for reclaiming local jobs at good wages is probably quite significant in the education and healthcare sectors. These are two sectors that I cited in my last lecture as good candidates for becoming more exportable. According to estimates from MAS' internal report in 2020, the health and education sector has an elasticity of substitution of 1.5, the highest among services industries. This means that if the wages of foreign workers in healthcare or education increase by 10 per cent, the demand for local workers as substitutes will increase by 15 per cent.

Not all jobs can benefit from technologically-driven productivity growth, but that does not mean that they cannot enjoy positive wage growth. Faster productivity growth in the tradable sectors, such as manufacturing and financial services, implies faster wage growth in those sectors. This increases demand for non-tradable services in the economy — such as food and beverage, healthcare and wellness, recreation and entertainment — which in turn means higher labour demand in these non-tradable sectors and higher wages. Economists call this the Balassa–Samuelson effect — the mechanism through which higher wages in the tradable sectors lead to higher wages in the non-tradable sectors as well. As the American economist Richard Baldwin puts it, the Balassa–Samuelson effect is one of the best forms of redistribution.[22] It is market-driven.

But in Singapore, we have blunted the Balassa–Samuelson effect through a large foreign worker intake in the non-tradable sector.

A strategy of tightening foreign labour supply to reclaim local jobs will likely have cost implications across society. If there were consolidation in the industry to achieve greater cost efficiencies, then it would not be inflationary. If there were productivity improvements through technology, the cost pass-through would be limited. But if the higher wages were not matched by higher productivity, then it would translate into higher costs, such as for healthcare and social services. It may well be that the government has to bear a larger fiscal burden to support some of these higher wages in the non-tradable sectors. That in and of itself is not a reason for perpetuating higher foreign worker dependency and low wages in these sectors. It means there are trade-offs that must be weighed carefully.

The key question for Singapore is: Do we want a dual economy with high inequality or a more inclusive society with higher wages but also higher costs? The Nordic countries have strict limits on low-wage foreign workers, which have facilitated a more equitable income distribution, low unemployment and a sustained commitment to productivity and innovation. If Singapore wants to be a bit more like the Nordic countries, it is not just government policies that would need to be adjusted but also the mindsets of businesses, citizens and workers. Firms must reduce their reliance on cheap labour, citizens must be prepared to pay more for better quality services and workers must be open to a greater variety of jobs. This brings us to the third escalator: making every job a professional job.

Escalator III: Professionalising Jobs

The key to understanding and beginning to address issues of income inequality is to look at differences in occupational wages at a granular level.

Why do many occupations in non-tradable domestic services pay so little in Singapore? Many of these jobs are paid less compared to advanced country norms. In some of these countries, professions that are not traditionally considered white-collar jobs are well paid relative to median wages. They also have favourable career development paths. Let me highlight two categories of jobs: *craftsmen and related trades,* and *health, education and social workers.*

Consider wages in four craftsmen type occupations — carpenter, electrician, welder and vehicle mechanic. Let us compare the latest median wages of these four occupations across Singapore, Australia, the US, and the UK relative to their respective estimated national median wages, represented by the horizontal line at 100 (Figure 4). In Singapore, carpenters and electricians are paid only 50 to 55 per cent of our median wage, whereas these occupations are paid at 100 per cent or more of the

Figure 4.   Median Wages of Craftsmen and Related Trades Occupations Relative to National Median Wages

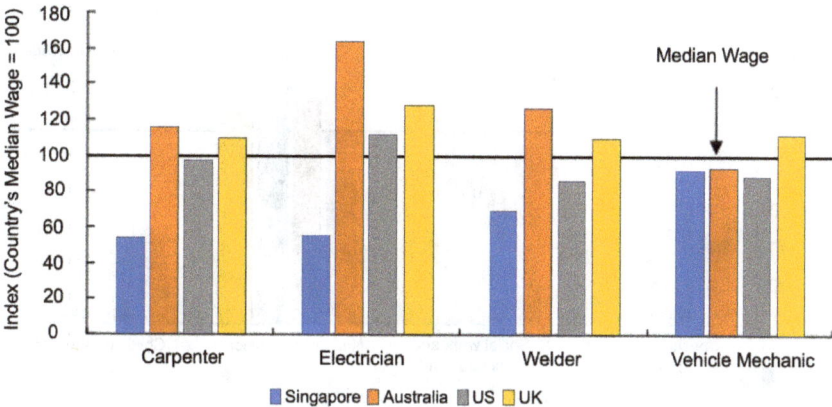

Source: Australia Taxation Office, "Taxation Statistics 2018–19 Individuals: Average and Median Taxable Income, Salary or Wages, and Total Income, by Occupation and Sex," accessed July 20, 2021, https://data.gov.au/data/dataset/taxation-statistics-2018-19/resource/47b26cb2-a680-444f-99ab-e94ed4ae9886?inner_span=True; U.S. Bureau of Labor Statistics, "May 2020 National Occupational Employment and Wage Estimates United States," accessed July 20, 2021, https://www.bls.gov/oes/current/oes_nat.htm; Office for National Statistics, United Kingdom, "Earning and Hours Worked, Industry by Four-Digit SIC: ASHE Table 16," accessed July 20, 2021, https://www.ons.gov.uk/employmentandlabourmarket/peopleinwork/earningsandworkinghours/datasets/industry4digitsic2007ashetable16; Ministry of Manpower, Singapore, "Occupational Wages 2020," accessed July 20, 2021, https://stats.mom.gov.sg/Pages/Occupational-Wages-Tables2020.aspx; MAS estimates.

median wage in Australia, the US and the UK. Our welders are paid better, at 70 per cent of the median wage, but still lower than in the other countries where welders are paid 85 to 125 per cent of the median wage. Our vehicle mechanics are paid well, at 90 per cent of the median wage, roughly similar to Australia and the US. Perhaps it is because our cars are so expensive and we take care of them so well that we are prepared to pay our vehicle mechanics handsomely?

Let us now look at four occupations in the healthcare, education and social services sector — special education teachers, social work professionals, nurses and childcare workers (Figure 5). Special education teachers are paid at 90 per cent of the median wage in Singapore, compared with 105 to 120 per cent of the median wage in the other three countries. Social work professionals are paid at close to 95 per cent of the median wage in

Figure 5.   Median Wages of Health, Education and Social Sector Occupations Relative to National Median Wages

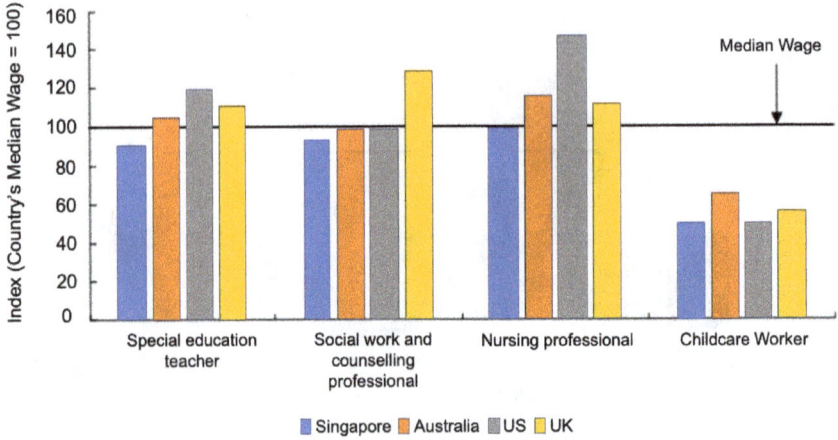

Source: Australia Taxation Office, "Taxation Statistics 2018–19 Individuals: Average and Median Taxable Income, Salary or Wages, and Total Income, by Occupation and Sex," accessed July 20, 2021, https://data. gov.au/data/dataset/taxation-statistics-2018-19/resource/47b26cb2-a680-444f-99ab-e94ed4ae9886?inner_ span=True; U.S. Bureau of Labor Statistics, "May 2020 National Occupational Employment and Wage Estimates United States," accessed July 20, 2021, https://www.bls.gov/oes/current/oes_nat.htm; Office for National Statistics, United Kingdom, "Earning and Hours Worked, Industry by Four-Digit SIC: ASHE Table 16," accessed July 20, 2021, https://www.ons.gov.uk/employmentandlabourmarket/peopleinwork/ earningsandworkinghours/datasets/industry4digitsic2007ashetable16; Ministry of Manpower, Singapore, "Occupational Wages 2020," accessed July 20, 2021, https://stats.mom.gov.sg/Pages/Occupational-Wages-Tables2020.aspx; MAS estimates.

Singapore, not far from Australia and the US, where it is closer to 100 per cent. Nurses in Singapore are paid at the median wage; in the UK and Australia they are paid 10 to 15 per cent higher than the median wage. Childcare workers are paid well below the median in all four countries. This is somewhat strange given how much people everywhere value their children.

Perhaps more striking than the statistics are the real-life stories. A Singaporean lady who wrote to me after my last lecture related how her friend who is a doctor in London working at the National Health Service (NHS) found that the Polish plumber fixing her home heating system had a higher income than her; in fact, he also went on better vacations and was giving her vacation tips! In Australia, visiting relatives, I have seen how the electrician drives to the customer's house in a car. He is well dressed, carries with him sophisticated equipment and goes about his task professionally. The median wage of an electrician in Australia is more than 60 per cent above the national median (Figure 4).

Income inequality is high because wages in many skilled blue-collar jobs in Singapore are low relative to the median wage, compared with other countries. In Singapore, many of these professions are not well paid or seen as promising careers: there is a social stigma against manual work and a reliance on low-wage foreign workers to fill these jobs.

One particular occupation that we should pay early attention to is long-term care providers. A 2018 study by the Lien Foundation on long-term care manpower benchmarked Singapore to four jurisdictions in Asia — Australia, Hong Kong, Japan and Korea — all with high-income, fast-ageing populations.[23] According to the report, despite concerted efforts to raise pay, redesign jobs and improve skills and productivity, the sector in Singapore seems afflicted by constant churn. There is heavy reliance on foreign workers: about 70 per cent of direct care workers in Singapore's nursing homes, day care centres and formal homecare settings are foreigners, compared with 32 per cent in Australia, less than 10 per cent in Japan and 5 per cent in Hong Kong and Korea.[24] Salaries of direct care workers here are lower than the tax-adjusted long-term care compensation in the other four jurisdictions, where these jobs enjoy a high status.[25]

Some efforts are underway to raise the status of skilled workers in domestic non-tradable sectors. Take for instance plumbers.

A 10-year operation and technology road map has been drawn up to prepare plumbing firms for the new economy. The Singapore Plumbing Society, the National Trades Union Congress and seven small and medium-sized enterprises (SMEs) have undertaken to transform the sector.[26] Plumbing is a skilled work; it must become a conscious career choice rather than a fallback option. In Australia, to become a plumber, there are minimum requirements — in formal certification, licensing, apprenticeship and work experience. Maybe there is something we can learn here.

In fact, should we not set a goal? Make all jobs in Singapore professional. This is not a slogan. To be professional means being qualified and practising in a defined area of work, and having expertise and a commitment to that area of practice. Should we not all aim to be professional in our work?

Professionalising the jobs of plumbers, cleaners, gardeners and other skilled workers will require a change in the nature of these jobs. We need to increase the skills content, leverage on technology, improve business processes and raise the quality of output. The cleaner of the future may be required to undertake basic maintenance, plumbing, changing of lights, landscaping and provide delivery services. This is already happening in London.

To professionalise all jobs, we could start by dropping from our vocabulary this category called PMET — professional, managerial, executive and technical jobs. If we cannot abolish it, then at least drop the "P" from the category: it suggests that other jobs are not professional. We should question the premise that all Singaporeans should aim to take up PMET jobs. Any population would house a distribution of skillsets, requiring a diversity of pathways that can lead to different types of excellence.

To be an inclusive society, we must value social and vocational skills as much as academic intelligence. In European countries, skilled trades provide a middle-class lifestyle for many workers; these jobs provide dignity and social status. We must do the same in Singapore. It is not just a matter of government policy, though policy can play a role. It is a whole-of-country effort.

Switzerland is a shining example of what it takes. At the question-and-answer session following my second lecture, Chng Kai Fong and I discussed Switzerland. What is it about Switzerland where every job is valued and there is such a premium on quality? A Swiss gentleman living in Singapore wrote to me after hearing the lecture.

Let me quote him:

> *Switzerland has cultivated for decades a tradition of formalised and certificated vocational training/apprenticeships. There is a diligently structured and formalised training course for almost every occupation, from nurses to plumbers, from salespersons to gardeners, from farmers to accountants, from truck drivers to bakers, from cooks to dental assistants, from instrument makers to hairdressers, from ski instructors to watchmakers and office clerks. There are about 250 vocational trainings that are certified by federal authorities.*

Another Swiss gentleman had this to say:

> *For non-white collar jobs to receive the appropriate recognition, it requires a triangular relationship: apprentice — company — customer. In Singapore, the above-described relationship among worker-company-customer seems to be missing. Instead of industry players in the non-white collar sectors taking a keen interest to develop a skilled workforce and hence raising the wages of the workers, the government is the party doing the heavy lifting. It is telling that the PWM has to be mandated.*

We must aim for a pervasive and persistent professionalism: a relentless quest for excellence in every job throughout the work life. That leads us to the fourth escalator: lifelong learning.

Escalator IV: Lifelong Learning

As Senior Minister Tharman Shanmugaratnam puts it: "We have a world-class school system … our challenge now is to complement that world-class school system by having one of the best systems of lifelong learning as part of that continuum. We must invest in this."[27]

Training and skills upgrading need to be integrated as part of work life, not an episodic luxury during lull periods. Every job should be examined for how it will change in the next two to three years, what skills are required and how we can train people in these jobs to upskill. Workforce transformation must become one of the core capabilities of any enterprise.

Is it unthinkable that every worker is allowed to take a paid six-month learning sabbatical between age 40 and 50? The need for continuous education is probably strongest for those in this age category, to re-equip them for the next phase of their careers, either in their same jobs or different jobs. So, why not take time off to pick up fresh skills or capabilities that will be relevant for their jobs in future? Obviously, we will have to address the question of how this will be paid for. We would also need a structured process with clear learning outcomes, otherwise the sabbatical might be spent on the golf course!

We have to make it possible for seniors to remain actively engaged at work and to learn new things. The pedagogy would have to be different. Repetition may be necessary. I am 57. I had to be briefed three times before I understood blockchains. For our senior workers, staying engaged at work and, very importantly, learning new things is also critical to staving off mental decline. It seems the neural networks of the brain are best served by learning entirely new things, not related things. I once asked a doctor if I should try learning a new language to help ward off the risk of dementia. He said, "No, you're good at languages. It won't help you much. You should try learning something that you are not good at, that your brain is not wired for." So, I have decided to learn to play the piano after I retire, since I have no musical talent whatsoever.

SkillsFuture spearheads Singapore's drive towards lifelong learning. It aims to invest in people throughout life, it involves funding, it involves a delivery infrastructure and it involves going into the community where people live. We are not doing too badly and other countries are seeking to learn from us. But we must learn from others too.

Denmark is probably the gold standard in lifelong learning. Danes learn from their time in kindergarten almost to the time they die. Children don't just learn, they learn to learn; and as adults they never stop learning. Denmark is among the top within the European Union (EU) with 25 per cent of Danes between 25 and 64 years of age participating in some kind of learning activity over the preceding four weeks.[28] This is most remarkable.

We would do well to remember the Latin phrase: *Non scholae sed vitae* — we learn not for school but for life.

For the Least Among Us

I have focused on jobs and wages as a means for economic opportunity and social inclusion. But there are groups for whom what I have said so far will not be enough.

We cannot become a truly inclusive society if we do not look out for the least among us — our aged destitute, our disabled, our special needs children and our migrant workers. In the interest of time, let me focus on migrant workers — specifically the work permit holders.

The migrant worker is the most vulnerable group in our workforce. The outbreak of COVID-19 in our worker dormitories last year shone a bright light on how our migrant workers lived and worked. Many Singaporeans were shocked and saddened to know of their conditions. There has been a generous outpouring of support from many Singaporeans for our migrant workers in their hour of need as the virus ravaged through the worker dormitories. Let us build on this collective sense of empathy to better understand our migrant workers and to provide better lives for them as part of an inclusive society.

Our migrant workers too are part of the Singapore Story. Millions of them have, over the decades, helped to build this country. They play a key role in our economy and society. Foreign work permit holders make up almost 25 per cent of our workforce. We see their work everywhere — our Mass Rapid Transit (MRT) stations, our Housing and Development Board (HDB) flats, our shopping malls, our office buildings, and so on. They clean our tables at hawker centres, they serve our food at restaurants, they look after us in our hospitals. We have nearly 250,000 migrant domestic workers labouring in our homes.[29] They clean, they cook and they take care of our young children and our elderly parents.

Our migrant workers face many struggles. Most migrant workers arrive in Singapore with a heavy load of debt. They have to pay a few thousand dollars to agents in order to get a job here and a substantial part of what they earn goes to pay off these debts. Their salaries are low and sometimes delayed or not even paid. Sometimes, the cost of training is deducted from their salaries. Some migrant workers are reported to be on 12-hour shifts.[30] In some cases, the food catered for these workers is neither healthy nor sufficient for the demands of the job. Some migrant workers do not get adequate medical leave to recover from serious injuries sustained at work despite the law providing for this. I have heard of instances where injured workers were forced to leave when their work permits expired, before their compensation claims were resolved.

As for migrant domestic workers, we read in the media cases of these workers being overworked, underfed and abused. Many migrant domestic workers shoulder a disproportionate amount of the emotional burden of caring for elderly patients.

The government has put in place various measures to enhance the welfare of our migrant workers. There are strict requirements in place for workplace safety and proper accommodation. Work injury compensation is mandatory, so are regular medical check-ups. Last year, the government moved swiftly to improve conditions in the dormitories. There are plans to build dormitories with better facilities and living conditions. A new system is being rolled out to provide primary healthcare for migrant workers.

Can the government do more? Yes, a couple of things more. For a start, we could ban the practice of transporting migrant workers at the back of goods vehicles; they are exposed to the elements and at risk of serious injury in the event of an accident. Yes, it will raise business costs. But the question we should ask ourselves is whether we would allow our own citizens to be transported this way. In 2008, an 8-year-old boy was hurled out of his school bus in a traffic accident. There was an outcry from parents, and within a year the government made it compulsory for all small school buses to be fitted with seat belts.

But more important than what the government can do is what the rest of society can do. The practices of many of our businesses that employ migrant workers must change. There are clear laws against many of the abuses that I have highlighted. The Ministry of Manpower (MOM) deploys a small army of officers to enforce these laws and check for abuses. Every year, MOM officers pick up dormitory operators in breach of licensing conditions. But MOM cannot be everywhere. There must be public vigilance against bad practices and pressure on errant businesses to change their ways.

Thankfully, there is growing awareness among Singaporeans about the plight of migrant workers. It is heartening that we have quite a few dedicated non-governmental organisations (NGOs) that look out for the welfare and interests of our migrant workers. If we are not in a position to help our migrant workers directly, let us support the work these NGOs do.

Simple expressions of acknowledgement and gratitude can help a lot. Perhaps communities can launch initiatives to thank the migrant workers who clean and maintain their neighbourhoods? For our foreign domestic workers, perhaps employers can invest a little to help them acquire useful skills they can use when they go back to their home countries?

How much are we willing to pay for an inclusive society? One of the themes that has run from my second lecture through to this lecture is that we have a sizeable part of the economy based on cheap labour, local and foreign, and quite often proposals to raise local wages or improve conditions for foreign workers is met with resistance: that it will put these businesses out, lead to lay-offs of local employees or lead to higher costs for Singaporeans. I do not want to trivialise these costs. But it is a test of how earnestly we want to be an inclusive society. Are we willing to share the burden? Are we willing to pay the price?

Let me close with what I believe was Singapore's finest hour as we battled COVID-19 last year. It was April 2020, and our migrant workers were facing a massive wave of infections and confined to their dormitories, living in fear and anxiety.

Prime Minister Lee Hsien Loong spoke to reassure the nation, and he spoke directly to our migrant workers:[31]

> *To our migrant workers, let me emphasise again: we will care for you, just like we care for Singaporeans. We thank you for your cooperation during this difficult period. We will look after your health, your welfare and your livelihood. We will work with your employers to make sure that you get paid, and you can send money home. And we will help you stay in touch with friends and family.*

PM Lee did not stop there. He went on to say:

> *Ramadan begins in a few days' time. We will make sure that arrangements are made for our Muslim workers. When Aidilfitri comes next month, we will celebrate with our Muslim friends, just as we celebrated the Indian New Year with our Indian friends last week. This is our duty and responsibility to you, and your families.*

Let me repeat that: "This is our duty and responsibility to you and your families." Duty and responsibility. I think PM was speaking for all Singaporeans: we have a duty and responsibility to our migrant workers. Last year, many Singaporeans answered that call of duty. It augurs well for an inclusive society.

Ultimately, a truly inclusive society requires a value system that places the welfare of our fellow human beings alongside our own. We can be an inspiring nation, driven by purpose and based on values. I will share my thoughts on this in my fourth and final lecture.

Notes

1. Martin Sandbu, *The Economics of Belonging* (New Jersey: Princeton University Press, 2020), 17–36.
2. OECD, "Gini: Disposable Income, Post Taxes and Transfers," [2004–2020 data], accessed July 20, 2021, https://stats.oecd.org/Index.aspx?DataSetCode=IDD;

Singapore Department of Statistics, "Gini Coefficient among Resident Employed Households (Including Employer CPF Contributions)," [2020 data], accessed July 20, 2021, https://tablebuilder.singstat.gov.sg/table/CT/17242; Data was computed and compared using the square root scale method for cross-country comparisons.

3. OECD, "P50/P10 Disposable Income Decile Ratio," [2004–2020 data], accessed July 20, 2021, https://stats.oecd.org/Index.aspx?DataSetCode=IDD; MAS estimates.

4. Nominal wage data is from the Ministry of Manpower's Comprehensive Labour Force Surveys on the Gross Monthly Income from Work (Excluding Employer CPF) of Full-Time Employed Resident Workers. Real wage growth data are MAS staff estimates, obtained from deflating nominal wage growth by All-Items CPI.

5. WISE, "Inequalities in Household Wealth and Financial Insecurity of Households," July 2021, https://www.oecd.org/wise/Inequalities-in-Household-Wealth-and-Financial-Insecurity-of-Households-Policy-Brief-July-2021.pdf.

6. Nicolas Woloszko and Orsetta Causa, "Housing and Wealth Inequality: A Story of Policy Trade-Offs," *VoxEU*, March 31, 2020, https://voxeu.org/article/housing-and-wealth-inequality-story-policy-trade-offs.

7. OECD, "The Role and Design of Net Wealth Taxes in the OECD," *OECD Tax Policy Studies*, no. 26 (2018): 16.

8. Alan Manning, "The Elusive Employment Effect of the Minimum Wage," *Centre for Economic Performance Discussion Paper*, no. 1428 (May 2016): 3.

9. Ministry of Manpower, "Services Sector: Work Permit Requirements," accessed July 20, 2021, https://www.mom.gov.sg/passes-and-permits/work-permit-for-foreign-worker/sector-specific-rules/services-sector-requirements.

10. Ministry of Manpower, "What is the Local Qualifying Salary (LQS)?" accessed July 20, 2021, https://www.mom.gov.sg/faq/work-pass-general/what-is-the-local-qualifying-salary.

11. Ministry of Manpower, "Factsheet — Workfare Income Supplement," https://www.mom.gov.sg/-/media/mom/documents/speeches/2010/factsheet---wis-(110310).pdf.

12. Workfare, Singapore, "Factsheet on Enhancements to the Workfare Income Supplement Scheme," February 2019, https://www.workfare.gov.sg/Press%20 Releases/Pages/PressRelease_Feb2019.pdf.

13. Ministry of Trade and Industry, "The Impact of the Workfare Income Supplement Scheme on Individuals' Labour Outcomes," August 12, 2014, https://www.mti. gov.sg/-/media/MTI/Legislation/Public-Consultations/2014/The-Impact-Of-The-Workfare-Income-Supplement-Scheme-on-Individuals-Labour-Outcomes/ fa_2q14.pdf, 30–31.

14. OECD, *The OECD Tax-Benefit Model for Canada: Description of Policy Rules for 2019* (Paris: OECD Publishing, 2020); OECD, *The OECD Tax-Benefit Model for Poland: Description of Policy Rules for 2020* (Paris: OECD Publishing, 2020).

15. A monopsony occurs when there is a sole or dominant employer in a labour market and many workers looking for employment in that market. In this setting, the monopsony employer has the market power to set wages, which can lead to lower wages when workers are paid less than their marginal revenue product.

16. Ministry of Manpower, "Speech by Minister for Manpower, Mrs Josephine Teo at Debate on President's Address," September 1, 2020, https://www.mom.gov. sg/newsroom/speeches/2020/0901-speech-by-minister-for-manpower-mrs-josephine-teo-at-the-debate-on-president-address.

17. Irene Y. H. Ng, Yiying Ng, and Po Choo Lee, "Singapore's Restructuring of Low-Wage Work: Have Cleaning Job Conditions Improved?" *The Economic and Labour Relations Review* 29, no. 3 (2018): 320.

18. Janice Lim and Jun Yuan Yong, "The Big Read: Undervalued and Underpaid, Singapore's Essential Services Workers Deserve Better," *Today*, June 13, 2020, https://www.todayonline.com/big-read/big-read-singapores-under-valued-essential-services-workers-how-pay-them-what-they-deserve.

19. Ministry of Manpower, Comprehensive Labour Force Survey, various issues; MAS estimates.

20. Ibid.

21. Ministry of Manpower, "Eligibility for S Pass," https://www.mom.gov.sg/passes-and-permits/s-pass/eligibility; Ministry of Manpower, "Median Gross Monthly Income from Work (Including Employer CPF) of Full-Time Employed

Residents Aged Fifteen Years and Over by Occupation and Age," June 2020, https://stats.mom.gov.sg/Pages/Gross-Monthly-Income-Tables2020.aspx.

22. Richard Baldwin, personal communication with Ravi Menon, April 27, 2017.

23. Lien Foundation, "Long Term Care Manpower Study," July 2018, http://www.lienfoundation.org/sites/default/files/Long%20Term%20Care%20Manpower%20Study%20FINAL_0.pdf, 15.

24. Ibid, 17.

25. Ibid, 20–21.

26. NTUC Training and Transformation, "NTUC Facilitates Cross-Sector Collaboration to Uplift, Transform and Grow the Plumbing Industry in the Next 10 Years," accessed July 20, 2021, https://trainandtransform.ntuc.org.sg/trainandtransform/Pages/Details.aspx?ItemId=32.

27. Tharman Shanmugaratnam, speech given to the Twelfth Parliament at the Debate on Annual Budget Statement, March 5, 2014, *Hansard Parliamentary Debates* 91 (2014).

28. European Commission, "Education and Training Monitor 2020: Figure 45: Adult (Aged 25–64) Participation in Learning, 4-Week Reference Period, 2010 and 2019," accessed July 20, 2021, https://op.europa.eu/webpub/eac/education-and-training-monitor-2020/en/chapters/chapter6.html.

29. Ministry of Manpower, "Foreign Workforce Numbers," [2020 data], accessed July 20, 2021, https://www.mom.gov.sg/documents-and-publications/foreign-workforce-numbers.

30. HOME, "Coming Clean: A Study on the Wellbeing of Bangladeshi Conservancy Workers in Singapore," August 2020, https://drive.google.com/file/d/1EqG-aQJjI29sw7cNKRB7M64N-sJh-M4z/view, 10.

31. Ministry of Foreign Affairs, "PM Lee on the COVID-19 Situation in Singapore," April 21, 2020, https://www.mfa.gov.sg/Overseas-Mission/Washington/Mission-Updates/2020/04/PM-Lee-on-the-COVID-19-Situation-in-Singapore-on-21-April-2020.

Question-and-Answer Session

Moderated by Ms Chua Mui Hoong

Mr Ravi Menon speaking with Ms Chua Mui Hoong at his Q&A session
Source: Jacky Ho for the Institute of Policy Studies

Chua Mui Hoong: Good afternoon and a very warm and special hello to all of you. Ravi, I just wanted to say, what a pleasure it was to read your draft earlier this afternoon and then to listen to you. And I must say, I was particularly struck by how bold and transformational many of your ideas are, because I mean, if they were implemented it amounts to a complete reworking of Singapore society. I was just wondering, as someone who is an important economic policymaker, I just wonder how much traction is there in terms of support for this kind of ideas? Also, your very broad agenda has many different moving parts. So, if we were to say you are going to be the socio-economic czar that's going to be in charge of implementing this, what would be one key area that you will focus on first?

Ravi Menon: Thanks for the question, Mui Hoong. I wouldn't say the ideas here, taken on their own, are transformative. Many of these ideas have been talked about in many circles, including in government circles. If there's anything new, it is that I have tried to put them together. They reflect my own personal convictions, but I offer them not as concrete answers, as I can't claim to have studied them in great depth. The aim is to have a conversation around these ideas. Implementing these ideas in and of itself is not very difficult. It is a question of public acceptance, buy-in from the business community and society. That is why I keep emphasising that while there are some government policies that ought to change, society and the economy also have to come together and change some things. By providing examples from other countries and pointing to the situation that we are in, I hope to promote such a discussion. So, how much traction there will be for these ideas is something we need to have a Singapore conversation over.

There is a tendency to think that government policies can solve many of our problems. It is not so. In many of the European countries that I mentioned, industry takes the lead. The public stands for a certain set of values that they want to see, and then the government works together with them. So I hope we have that kind of conversation and compact. And if we do that and there is convergence — and it need not be around the ideas that I presented — then we will have a way forward.

Ms Chua: That is really interesting. Essentially, if we were to join the dots in terms of what your proposals amount to, we would end up with an alternative Singapore, a Singapore that is very different. It would be a high-wage, high-productivity, high-cost society. And the way we would go about getting to that place is to have a minimum wage floor at the bottom, tighten foreign workers' supply, reclaim jobs for locals, professionalise all jobs, and so on. I must say, personally, this appeals very much to the inner socialist in me. But I do wonder what the SMEs or business owners will be saying about this, as well as the workers.

I noticed that some questions are coming in, and there's a certain strain in them. Quite many of our listeners are asking, what would be the impact of this kind of high-wage economy on workers? Would it translate to high prices? Would the inflation outpace whatever wage increases they may get as they transit to professional jobs? Basically, who's going to bear the cost of such a high-wage society?

Mr Menon: Those are very good questions. Those are exactly the issues we need to investigate further. As I said, moving from a low-wage equilibrium to a high-wage equilibrium is a tricky transition. You can expect a fair amount of disruption and dislocation in the process. But I think, given how well Singapore has innovated in so many areas, this is not beyond our capability. And if you look at the small European countries who have done this well, it gives you a basis for thinking that we can too.

As costs and prices go up, wages are also going up, and so most people should be able to afford this. This is what you see in Switzerland and Denmark — people at the lower percentiles are able to afford many things that are highly priced because they still earn a decent wage. Now, of course, not everybody's wages is going to go up that way. There will be a segment, and in particular in healthcare, where I think the cost increase may not be small — if you pay your nurses well, reduce foreign worker dependence, use more technology in healthcare. Many may be able to afford it because they themselves have higher wages, working in other non-tradable sectors. But I suspect there will be quite a number who will not be able to afford it. This is where the state needs to come in and provide fiscal support.

So, if we want to reduce the number of nurses in Singapore, and in the process, raise wages of nurses substantially above the median, which is the case in other countries, you will have quite a large number of people entering the profession with pride. It will be a good middle-class job and pathway for many. Then, maybe the bottom 20 per cent will not be able to afford the higher healthcare costs. So the question is: Is it better for the government to help this group in a targeted manner, so that we can make this transition? Again, this is what the Europeans do. We do need a safety net for the people at the bottom so as to push mid-level wages up, which will push costs up. As I mentioned in my last lecture, one man's wage is another man's cost, and wage is the biggest part of any company's cost structure.

The current situation is not satisfactory. We have a dual economy. It is not as bad as in some other countries, but we have 35 per cent of GDP in sectors with high productivity growth and high wage growth, and the rest of the economy at much slower growth. Fortunately, we are still registering positive wage growth overall, but the gap is widening. At the bottom, we have a large number of foreign workers and low-wage Singaporeans side by side. This is the price — if we want to reduce inequality and resolve this dual economy, or at least reduce its degree, then we need to bear higher costs and higher prices, and help those who cannot bear the higher prices. But if we end up in a situation where we have to increase government subsidies for a large number of the population, then the policy has failed and it is not worth doing. Now, we cannot predict these things. But we should study them dispassionately, look at the evidence and facts, make some reasonable judgements, take small steps and learn along the way. If it does not pan out the way you expect, adjust your course. But I think we should move; we need to move. The current situation is not good; it traps too many people in low wages.

Ms Chua: We have one very graphic question on this issue. So one of the questioners asked, Singaporeans are very proud of our local food. How would you define a professional cook: somebody who has a degree, or somebody whose char kway teow is popular? And fundamentally, do you think Singaporeans are prepared to pay $15 for a plate of char kway teow at a hawker centre?

Mr Menon: Excellent question. It is a question I ask myself often. Why is it that so many of us are willing to step into a restaurant or a hotel and pay

$15 to $20 for chicken rice or char kway teow, which is actually not as good as the one you can get in the hawker centre at $3 or $4.

Prices are an outcome of demand and supply. Demand is a function of our willingness to pay. We've gotten so used to paying $3 for a plate of chicken rice that if the hawker raises it to $3.50, we get upset. Yet, once a month we go to a restaurant and we spend much more. Our hawker fare should fetch higher wages because the quality of the food is good. I mean, our hawker culture is now a United Nations Educational, Scientific and Cultural Organization (UNESCO) heritage. We must support it. This means we need to be prepared to pay more to keep it viable. In extreme, I would rather that the price for char kway teow goes up to $8, most of us happily and willingly pay for it and for the few who cannot afford it, we give them assistance. It is the better outcome if you have to provide assistance only to a small group, and the rest of us have high enough wages to pay one another for goods and services. It can be a virtuous cycle, because when I have high wages and I pay more for your services, you get higher wages and you are able to afford more things.

Ms Chua: I suppose another impact of high wages might be how it could affect our cost competitiveness. So, there is a question here on whether the professionalisation of traditionally blue-collar jobs in non-tradable sectors will affect the competitiveness of our tradable sectors as Singaporean workers pivot towards the former. How can we maintain a sustainable balance?

Mr Menon: Another very good question. These are issues we need to study very deeply. But let us not take as a given the past paradigm. There is a strong psyche across businesses, workers and government, which is overly sensitive to cost increases. I think it has got to do with the sudden recession the Singapore economy went through in 1985, when we were taken by surprise by how far we had let our cost structure get out of hand. As an economist I know that for a small open economy, we must always watch our real effective exchange rate, our relative unit labour costs and our exports must be competitively priced. That has not changed.

But we are now a different economy from 1985. If you look at the experience of advanced economies, they pay their workers good wages and sell their products in international markets at high prices; they are able to sell them because the quality is high. As consumers, we know we are willing to pay more if the quality and service are high. I think, in many regards, the quality in our tradable sector is world class. We are able to sell. The price will go up a little, there will be some loss of market share, but on balance, we have to weigh: are we still competitive? Our competitiveness must come from higher skills content, higher productivity, superior technology and better service. Cost matters, but I think it matters less than it did 30 years ago.

Ms Chua: There should not be a disincentive for us to raise wages?

Mr Menon: We should not jump to the conclusion that wage increases will automatically pass through to cost and price increases that will undermine competitiveness. We have already seen cost increases, and we are still able to compete.

Ms Chua: You made some very interesting suggestions on minimum wage. There's a question here from Professor Tommy Koh, who agrees that we should have both a minimum wage and PWM. The question is: What should be the minimum wage? According to some scholars and statisticians, this should be around $1,300. Does this sound right to you? I would also like to add on one other question on minimum wage. You mentioned that you went from yes to no and then back to yes, essentially. I was just wondering, what was the main factor that led you to say yes this time?

Mr Menon: The specific level of the minimum wage is not something I have studied deeply. However, I think the kinds of numbers that have been talked about, between $1,000 and $1,500, would seem about right. I think below $1,000, you're not likely to help many people. At the same time, I would be nervous if we got closer to $1,500. I know there is sympathy for something close to that level, because it does not seem a large amount of money for many in the middle class. But we have to look carefully at the number of workers who are currently making well below that in wages, and not put them at risk of unemployment. You can force a minimum wage, but you cannot force employment. The empirical literature gives us some confidence that you can have a minimum wage without causing unemployment, provided you do not set it too high. As a conservative civil servant I would start with something lower, watch how things are panning out, see if we can manage the dislocations and then maybe increase it later on. It is also important to announce any such move well in advance so that businesses can adjust. And tell them, "Look, we do not want you to shed workers, but improve your processes and consolidate your operations so that you can afford to pay this minimum wage in time." I know I have not answered the question on a number for the minimum wage but I think it needs careful thought. The discussions in Singapore on the minimum wage do not seem to fully appreciate the intricacies involved.

Why did I change my mind on the minimum wage three times? When I left university as a young economist, I thought the minimum wage was a bad idea. It is classic microeconomics — when you set a floor that is above what the market would clear at, you will create a surplus, in this case, unemployment. The theory is very clear on what will happen. So I thought this was quite a bad idea.

Then, over the next many years, I studied the empirical literature. Alan Manning puts it very well — there are lots of studies trying to find the unemployment effects of minimum wage. But it is elusive, they cannot find it. The studies mostly find that when the minimum wage is imposed or when it is increased, it gets passed on to the workers. There is hardly any cutback in employment, prices increase a bit and profits go down and absorb the higher wages, the extent of which varies across sectors and industries. There are no doubt a few studies that have found some unemployment effects, so we cannot over-generalise. But it gave me more confidence — not from the theoretical point of view that I started with, but from the empirical literature — that if we design a minimum wage well, it could work. It could help more than it hurts.

Then years later, I changed my mind again and thought that the minimum wage was not such a good idea after all. This was mostly for political economy reasons. You can design a rational and reasonable minimum wage. But if you look at what has happened in many countries, the minimum wage becomes politicised and there are continuous pressures to raise it. That is when the discipline is lost. I think in some European countries, the minimum wage is close to or at the point at which its adverse effects on employment outweigh the benefits. There are proposals in the US currently to dramatically raise the minimum wage. In my view, it is going too far. I think the quantum of increase is not going to be helpful to many segments of the economy, but unfortunately the debate has become politicised. So, for political economy reasons, I thought it is better not getting into all that; focus on the PWM, focus on WIS, and do not focus on a minimum wage.

More recently, I changed my mind again. I have more confidence that Singapore can do this well. We have a very strong tripartite mechanism; workers, employers and the government can sit together and come to an understanding on how we will design a minimum wage and how future increases can be based on a sound framework or formula. We have formulas for electricity prices, we have formulas for water tariffs and we even have formulas for ministerial salaries. I am sure we can come up with a decent formula for minimum wage adjustments. But we must maintain that trust among the tripartite parties to keep the process sound.

So, more recently, I have come back to saying yes to a minimum wage, because I think if any country can do this well, Singapore can. But again, I say this without studying the full economic effects: prices, wages, employment, and these effects vary across different sectors. So first, we need to put aside ideology and conventional wisdom, look at the data, look at the facts and debate dispassionately, and come to a consensus. I think we can pull it off. Right now, I'm a yes for the minimum wage, but I might change my mind again in the future!

Ms Chua: Might this be one of the low-hanging fruits that you could help pluck?

Mr Menon: I do not think so. Of all the elements in the job and wage architecture I described — the two safety nets, the one trampoline and the four escalators — the minimum wage will probably help the least number of people: those whose wages are at the 20th percentile and a little above. Of course, they need to be helped because our ratio of wages at the 20th percentile to the 50th percentile is low by international standards.

But the more impactful measure will be to get the progressive wage model expanded, much more broadly than today. There are plans and there is a commitment to do that. So, I'm not sure I would describe the minimum wage as a low-hanging fruit, especially given all the unfortunate controversy that has built up around it. I still think it is a good idea. But, if you want to do things faster to impact more people, the PWM might be a better measure to focus on. We can also look at how we can improve the WIS.

I would also really like to explore this idea of professionalising every job, to set that as a national goal. It is not a low-hanging fruit, but in fact it is the ultimate fruit. I shared in my lecture what the Swiss gentleman sent me, about the wide range of jobs in Switzerland that require certification, licensing, apprenticeship and continuous learning. It is inspiring. I would go for that, but that is not low-hanging. But we have got to start doing that now so that in five to 10 years' time, we will get there.

Ms Chua: There is somebody watching who is very keen on this. He says: I like the idea of making PMET "P" only. Who can take the lead to start this process or movement? How does one even go about something so major?

Mr Menon: Well, the PMET category is our own invention. In the international classifications used in labour statistics, there is a category called professional, another category for managerial, another for services, and so on. This is international convention, it has not changed for many decades, we have adopted it and what we did actually is to combine these four things together.

Ms Chua: You mean PMET is a Singapore invention?

Mr Menon: PMET is a Singapore invention of sorts, by putting these categories together. Not all of us can become managers or executives, not all of us are going to be technicians or tech-savvy. So, we can accept that for some jobs, these are proper definitions. But what is a professional? Isn't a nurse a professional? Isn't a plumber a professional? A professional is someone who excels in his profession.

Doing away with the PMET category has symbolic and signalling value. If there is appetite, we could do it. Again, I am looking for a conversation around this. I am sure some people will be able to come up with reasons why dropping PMET might not be a good idea. We need to listen to those views, but I have just put that thought out there, and ultimately it is for the government and Ministry of Manpower to decide.

Ms Chua: Now, just thinking beyond the signalling effect, how might you actually go about professionalising these domestic services? You mentioned plumbing, that there is a timeline and an entire framework. So would you have to go sector by sector and look at the job requirements and so on?

Mr Menon: We have to look at this occupation by occupation. I think we spend too much time in our public discourse and national discussions looking at Gini coefficients and the P ratios. But those are income outcomes. Where do incomes come from? They come from jobs and occupations. It's a lot more insightful to look at occupational wages and try to understand how they are determined in the way they are. My staff at MAS helped me pick these eight occupations and did this comparison of relative median wages across countries. We should do this for every occupation, and for each of them seek to understand why there is variance. There may be good reasons; we should not just say, "Because Australia pays so much, we should pay so much." There may be good reasons — the demand and supply situation could be different. But we need to understand these things.

If you take jobs such as plumbing and electricians, you will find that today, these are jobs that we do not formally train for. There is a wide variety in standards. As a customer, because you do not know what you are getting, you tend not to pay much. Why does it work well in hairdressing? Hairdressers are paid well relative to the median because there is a transparent skills ladder: trainee, stylist, senior stylist, and so on, with different price points.

We need to have that for electricians, we need to have that for plumbers and gardeners. The Swiss have done it, and some smaller European countries have done it. We too can. But it is hard work — there is no silver bullet. It is not like a minimum wage increase. This is going occupation by occupation to build a skills ladder. But if we do this well, we can professionalise every job, and make the drive for excellence an important ingredient of every job.

Ms Chua: That sounds inspiring. There is a question here about the Gini coefficient that you just mentioned, from Ravi Philemon, who is the Secretary-General of the Red Dot United. You pointed out that the Gini Coefficient is not a sufficient measure of inequality. Similarly, GDP may not be a good measure of human well-being. Are we on the right path by using, and maybe overly relying, on GDP as a planning tool?

Mr Menon: We do not rely on GDP as a be-all and end-all planning tool. It is just the one that gets the most attention from the government, media and popular commentary. The most important variable, I would say, is the rate of growth in median wages. A major reason why the consensus in favour of the market is breaking down in advanced countries is the stagnation of the middle class. The importance of the middle class to a policy goes back to the wisdom of Aristotle — that if the middle do not feel confident of their future, democracy suffers. Therefore, we need to ensure that real median wages continue to grow well. So far, we have achieved that. This is why I think, broadly, things are okay in Singapore. We have a low-wage worker problem, quite a serious one, but at the median we are doing well. We need to sustain it; it is not easy. All the more, we need to professionalise our jobs. More than GDP, I would look at median wage growth.

But GDP growth is a good indicator, and is a major enabler of median wage growth. People who criticise GDP growth need to examine what the alternatives are. Actually, what you need is a mix of a few indicators, which is what the government does. The Ministry of Finance puts out the Singapore Public Sector Outcomes Review reports, which look at a whole range of indicators, and GDP is just one of them. Inflation, wage growth and human indices are all important. We have to look at about five to 10 indices that describe, collectively, human welfare. GDP is just one of them, and it is a good enabler for many of the other metrics.

In terms of median wage growth, Singapore has done better in the last decade than in the previous. A lot of it has to do with GDP growth. Because GDP growth was good, and because it also happened to be widespread, and a good part of it from 2015 onwards came from productivity growth, median wages held up at the median well. GDP is a necessary condition but not sufficient condition for healthy median wages. Let us neither discard GDP growth nor worship it as if it alone mattered.

Ms Chua: There are a couple of questions here on the friction when that happens, when the economy is going through transformation and disruption: We all have educated friends and family members who have been displaced or furloughed due to COVID-19 and ended up in low-barrier jobs, such as becoming private hire drivers. How do we persuade them to rescale and reinvent themselves so that they are on a more stable future career path? Another related question about automation and how they may end up getting rid of entire jobs. Although the safety net is good, given how difficult it may be for them to transit to new jobs, is there a role for the government in matching them to future jobs?

Mr Menon: This goes back to the trampoline that I mentioned. I would like to call it re-employment support, rather than unemployment benefits, because when people in their mid-40s to late 40s and early 50s get displaced, they are caught in a bind. There are several reasons. One, although they are usually at above median wage, it is not as if they have a lot of savings. Two, some of the people in this group have large housing mortgages. Some of them have school-going children. Some of their children are entering university, so that's more expensive. They have fixed outlays that limit their mobility and flexibility once they are displaced. As their financial resources are limited, they are in a hurry to get another job and start earning.

And this is where I think we can take a leaf from Denmark, because people are not afraid to move from one job to another. Or if they are displaced from one and move to another, they have time to prepare. People need time to look for what fits their inclinations and their aptitudes, to learn new skills and build capabilities, to go for an attachment or course.

The problem here is that many may suffer a financial loss if they were to take their time for the next job. And so, some form of re-employment support would be useful because it takes off some of the risks that they're bearing. For instance, if I need eight months to prepare and find a job and do not have a regular income, how will I service my mortgage? How will I send my kids to university? How will I pay their tuition fees? Some kind of re-employment support would be useful.

I am laying it out as simply a concept, and there is nothing innovative about it. The devil's in the details, what should be the replacement ratio? If you were drawing $8,000 a month, do we support up to $8,000? Now that is going to be very expensive. Who is going to pay for it? There has got to be some sharing between the employer and the government. It has to be time-bound. One of the abuses of such programmes that you see in many countries is people who cook up all kinds of paperwork to show the authorities that they are looking for a job, when they are not seriously looking or training. So, we would need a whole structure to make sure that people are picking up relevant skills with a career pathway in mind. In

SkillsFuture, we have the basic ingredients for many of this already, such as the Professional Conversion Programmes and Attach and Train Programmes. We need to scale them.

Ms Chua: I am just curious on this particular re-employment assistance scheme. Where do you stand conceptually? Are you in favour of something that is funded primarily by the worker themselves with the employer? Or one that is pooled by some kind of insurance?

Mr Menon: I will state in general terms. What generally works well, and what economists would call incentive-compatible, is something that involves skin in the game from all the stakeholders involved. It cannot be that the worker does not put in anything. He has to demonstrate commitment, the employer has to put in something, and the state has to put in something. What the ratios will be, those are the details that need to be worked on. But I think as a principle there must be burden sharing, to make sure that we can help workers in their 40s and 50s who are at risk of displacement, make these job and career switches. It is not an easy task.

Ms Chua: I am very curious, given that you are a central banker — in many ways, many of your broad proposals for socio-economic change were a little bit unexpected. I am just very curious as to what values underpinned your thinking when it comes to proposing such a change in architecture for Singapore?

Mr Menon: As I said, I do not think I have said anything very bold or transformative.

Ms Chua: Taken together, the whole is greater than the sum of its parts. What values underpin that kind of thinking?

Mr Menon: I have called this series *The Singapore Synthesis* because it brings together values from across the spectrum. The primary value is that people must be self-reliant as much as possible. The paradox is that the government needs to help people become self-reliant. The traditional left and right divide does not make any sense. The right says people must be self-reliant; if you take care of them, they will become dependent and entitled. The left says no, they cannot take care of themselves, the state has to take care of them. This is an endless oversimplified debate.

Over the years, I have come to the conclusion that you cannot leave things entirely to the market. And yet, we have seen so much of how state welfarism has damaged societies, such as the will to work, the incentive to work and one's sense of self-esteem and self-worth. In a nutshell, the value that underpins much of what I have said is about a work-centred social security model, a work-centred inclusion model, because work means you help yourself, but you need help from the state, from the community and from employers to be able to exercise that self-reliance. You will need safety nets if you fall and mechanisms that help you bounce back, because these things happen.

That is the kind of synthesis of values of self-reliance and public support that we need. We cannot ignore inequalities in our society. We cannot look the other way. We need to come together. And when we say government, we should always remember, it is taxpayers. This is why it is all about collective societal sharing. The question for taxpayers is this: Can we do more to help our fellow Singaporeans become more self-reliant? So, if you need to have a re-employment scheme, it needs to be paid for in part at least by the government, which means taxpayers. It is also about solidarity, which is another value that underpins much of what I have said, that all parties need to chip in, such as in helping migrant workers, we did not talk very much about that, but all of us need to chip in, not just the government. I will come back to this theme in my fourth lecture.

Ms Chua: We look forward to that inspiring lecture. Thank you everyone.

Lecture IV

AN INSPIRING NATION

Innovation and Inclusion

L et me briefly take stock of the discussion so far before I move on to the theme of this last lecture, "An Inspiring Nation".

The four horsemen — Demographics, Inequality, Technology and Climate — will bring about profound economic and societal changes. To manage these tectonic shifts, seize the opportunities and build a better future, we need to be much more of an innovative economy and an inclusive society.

I have shared several ideas, taking care to also highlight the trade-offs and challenges in each of them: make our domestic services exportable, digitalise our economy end-to-end, green our economy, attract global talent while growing the Singaporean core, study a minimum wage, enhance Workfare Income Supplement, broaden progressive wages, reclaim domestic services jobs for locals, professionalise all jobs, inculcate lifelong learning and look after the least among us. And I made a special pitch for our migrant workers. I thank all those who have written to me with words of encourage-ment and support as well as alternative views.

Underpinning the specific ideas are the three broad themes of Innovation, Inclusion and Inspiration. The Singapore Synthesis is about how we can harness these themes in a mutually reinforcing way. At the heart of all innovation must be the desire for inclusion, to make people's lives better. To enhance inclusion, we need innovation in our thinking and mental models. Underpinning both innovation and inclusion must be a set of values and sense of purpose that gives us the inspiration to give our best, to overcome our obstacles and to build a better Singapore.

Innovation must become one of the defining features of Singapore, the way meritocracy, multiracialism, trust and stability are. Singapore is making its way up in the international technology league tables. Just one example: in a survey of 800 tech leaders by KPMG, Singapore was the number one preferred technology hub outside Silicon Valley.[1] I personally think the ranking is rather generous. But there is no question that Singapore is gaining mindshare as one of the most digitally advanced countries in the world. Let us apply that same innovative spirit to make our education and healthcare services the Oxbridge and Mayo of Asia respectively, and propel Singapore as the vanguard of a green revolution for a more sustainable Asia. I believe we have the potential but are still far from realising it. We need to raise our level of ambition.

Innovation is ultimately about optimism and hope for the future. It requires a certain restlessness of the spirit, a sense of adventure, and a daringness to take calculated risks. It is not about technology or rocket science. It is a passion for continuous improvement in everything we do.

Inclusion too must become one of the attributes people think of first when they think of Singapore. True inclusion is more multifaceted than simple measures of inequality like the Gini coefficient.

Focusing on the more important dimensions of inclusion, the picture is mixed. Singapore is doing well on median wages, not doing well at the level of the low-wage workers. The wealth gap is probably widening but may be not as bad as in some other advanced countries. Social mobility has been good so far but could come under pressure in the future.

I want to emphasise real median wages because it is critical that the broad middle of society is doing well. Middle class stagnation is at the root of the social discontent and political polarisation afflicting many advanced countries. I am mentioning this number for the third time because I think it is so important: real median wages in Singapore increased by an average of 2.6 per cent per annum from 2011 to 2020.[2]

Partly because our broad middle has done well and not stagnated like in other countries, the gap between our 20th percentile and the median is higher than in other countries. Our low-wage workers are caught in low productivity, low labour cost business models, mostly in domestic non-tradable services. Hence the focus in my last two lectures on uplifting the domestic services sectors.

Although we are doing okay on social mobility, this is the area that bears closest attention. Our current generations are doing better than their parents because we were in transit from Third World to First World. Going forward, it is going to be tougher. Our top priority for the social inclusion agenda must be to ensure that every child from a low-income or vulnerable family gets a good start in life.

Now, coming to inspiration, by which I mean the values and sense of purpose that guide us as a nation. Many of the issues we have discussed are not straightforward; they are laden with trade-offs and uncertainty. There is a risk to bear to become a more innovative economy. There is a price to pay to create a more inclusive society. Evidence-based analysis and a judicious weighing of options will take us some of the way in making these decisions. But ultimately, the choices boil down to what society values as important: who we are, and what we stand for.

A Values-Based and Purpose-Driven Nation

An inspiring nation is one that is based on values and driven by purpose.

There is a misperception that Singapore has been guided too strongly by economic perspectives at the expense of social and other considerations. Economics is not about dollars and cents; it is about scarcity and choice.

Because resources are limited, we cannot have more of everything; we have to choose. This entails weighing costs and benefits, and making trade-offs among competing ends, which is what most public policies are about. Some costs and benefits can be quantified, many others cannot be measured easily. But in making any decision, we are implicitly imputing a value to the benefits and costs of different options. Sound economic analysis helps us to be clear about these costs and benefits. Which particular option we choose depends on judgements. Economics cannot tell us what our judgements should be; they depend ultimately on our values.

Values are different from value. As Mark Carney, former governor of the Bank of England, explains it in a recent lecture:

> *Value is the regard that something is held to deserve, its importance, its worth, its usefulness. Value isn't necessarily constant but, rather, specific to time and situation.... Values represent principles or standards of behaviour, they are judgements of what is important in life, such as fairness, responsibility, sustainability, solidarity, dynamism, resilience and humility.*[3]

Focusing on values can help to clarify many of our tough choices. We have discussed many of such choices in the last two lectures. Beyond quantifiable costs and benefits, which are important, the answer to the question of how far we should raise carbon taxes depends at least in part on how importantly we regard, as a core value, doing our part as a global citizen in the effort to secure a sustainable future. Likewise, reducing the intake of low-wage foreign workers to reclaim jobs for Singaporeans will mean an increase in cost that the rest of society must shoulder. The cost–benefit analysis will provide the numbers but it cannot provide the answer. That depends on values. If we want to move towards a society where all jobs are done with professionalism and pride, then more important than the monetary value we place on the job are the values we hold about the dignity of all work.

Focusing on values can inspire more socially altruistic behaviour. Values appeal to our better instincts; they inspire us to make more altruistic choices.

Using monetary value as an incentive does have its usefulness but it does not bring out the best in us. The American psychologist Barry Schwartz who wrote the seminal book *The Paradox of Choice* tells the story of how Switzerland held a referendum many years ago on where to site its nuclear waste dumps.[4] People in two cantons were asked if they would accept a nuclear dump in their communities. Although people thought such dumps might be dangerous and might decrease property values, 50 per cent of those who were asked said they would accept one. People felt their responsibility as Swiss citizens. But when people were asked if they would accept a nuclear waste dump if they were paid a substantial sum of money each year, a remarkable thing happened. Only about 25 per cent of respondents agreed.[5] The offer of cash effectively undermined the motive to be a good citizen; it ended up making a public interest decision one of self-interest.

A growing body of work in social psychology highlights the difference between intrinsic motivations and external ones. Intrinsic values such as moral conviction or passion for the task at hand inspires superior outcomes, compared with external motivations such as money or other tangible rewards. Excessive reliance on monetary incentives to promote good behaviour will not have durable outcomes. An inspiring nation is one that appeals to the higher virtues and instincts in us.

Focusing on values such as resilience, sustainability and delayed gratification can promote long-term orientation and reduce short-termism. We tend to value the present much more than the future. Most people do not save enough for their retirement not because they cannot afford to, but because they value present consumption much more than future consumption. Is the preoccupation with the present the reason why societies are not doing enough to reduce their carbon emissions, even though actions today will be less costly than those required in the future?

Likewise, to promote innovation, we need to promote a value system that emphasises constant questioning over an unthinking conformity. This must start from a young age, so that as children grow up, they can think in original ways.

People are inspired when they focus on something larger than themselves. It could be the community around them, unborn future generations, their country, the environment or the planet. Let us encourage and celebrate such other-centredness.

Our values should draw the best from across different traditions. Let us not fall into the trap that many countries have: where values are defined solely by ideology or political persuasions. As Senior Minister Tharman Shanmugaratnam puts it:

> *The traditional strategies of both left and right in the advanced societies have lost their appeal. But we need more than ever the core values of the left, of social empathy and solidarity. We also need the core ethic of personal responsibility and effort that the conservatives have always espoused. These values are not at odds with each other.*[6]

And that, I would add, is the essence of the Singapore Synthesis: to imbibe a set of values that draws the best from multiple perspectives.

Let me share my thoughts on five values-based attributes that could make Singapore an inspiring nation — to Singaporeans as well as others:

- A meritocracy of hope
- A beacon for diversity
- A city of giving
- A heart for the environment
- A thousand points of light

A Meritocracy of Hope

Let me begin with a meritocracy of hope.

There are three vital institutions that have underpinned the growth of countries that today we regard as developed: democracy, meritocracy and the market. They have also been key success factors for Singapore's own development as a nation, a society and as an economy. Underlying democracy, meritocracy and the market is a set of common values: freedom, fairness, equality, excellence, to name a few. These values have helped to shape the ethos, policies and social compact in many of these countries.

Today, all three institutions are under pressure in many parts of the advanced world. In many countries, democracy is not working as well as it used to, with gridlock in government, growing polarisation of views and excessive focus on rights without due regard to responsibilities. Meritocracy is coming under growing criticism as being stacked in favour of those already at the top and failing to deliver the equality of opportunity that is one of its central premises. Likewise, many people are questioning whether the market economy is indeed delivering the optimal outcomes that its proponents claim; unfettered markets are seen as having contributed to financial crises, monopolistic practices and grossly unequal outcomes.

There is something about democracy, meritocracy and the market that, if left completely unfettered, lead to excesses that are socially harmful. At least for the market economy, this is probably what Karl Marx had in mind when he predicted that capitalism contains within itself "the seeds of its own destruction".[7]

But there is no better alternative to democracy, meritocracy and the market. As Winston Churchill once said, "Democracy is the worst form of government except for all those other forms that have been tried from time to time."[8] The same could be said of the market economy and meritocracy. We need to continually refine, temper and even constrain, to some extent, democracy, meritocracy and the market, so that we can continue to harness their benefits while minimising their excesses. Marx's prediction did not come true because capitalism continually reinvented itself, or rather governments intervened in many ways over the last 200 years to make markets work better.

Likewise, meritocracy is at risk of becoming rigid or hereditary if growing inequality of outcomes leads to a growing inequality of opportunities. This is not the fault of meritocracy per se but the outcome of very natural human instincts, namely, what the Irish author Lucinda

Riley calls "the most powerful force on earth" — "the love of a parent for a child."[9] As I mentioned in my first lecture, people are naturally good at passing on their privileges to their children. But when the elite reproduce themselves, we are at risk of a hereditary meritocracy. To use Marx's analogy, meritocracy, when carried to an extreme, undermines itself and sows the seeds of its own destruction. So, every now and then, meritocracy needs to be saved from itself. It is not easy for public policies alone to do this — after all, policy is up against "the most powerful force on earth". We need a whole-of-society effort to fine-tune our meritocracy. Again, it comes down to values.

Can we have a more enlightened meritocracy — a meritocracy that offers hope? Our meritocracy has worked reasonably well so far. But the risks of an increasingly narrow and rigid meritocracy are real. Can we redefine and enhance our meritocracy so that it remains an expander of opportunity, not a restrictor? Let me highlight three ways how we might do this:

- A broad meritocracy — to recognise a more diverse set of human talents and skills
- An inclusive meritocracy — to blunt some of the sharp edges of meritocracy
- A compassionate meritocracy — to recognise the role that society and fortune play in the success of individuals

First, a broad meritocracy. Isaac Asimov, the famous science fiction writer and professor of biochemistry, had an IQ of 160; that put him well into the genius range. In an endearing passage in his autobiography, Asimov says:

Suppose my auto-repair man devised questions for an intelligence test. Or suppose a carpenter did, or a farmer, or, indeed, almost anyone but an academician. By every one of those tests, I'd prove myself a moron, and I'd be a moron, too. In a world where I could not use my academic training and my verbal talents but had to do something intricate or hard, working with my hands, I would do poorly. My intelligence, then, is not absolute but is a function of the society I live in and of the fact that a small subsection of that society has managed to foist itself on the rest as an arbiter of such matters.[10]

The recognition that we must broaden our definitions of merit and recognise excellence in different areas has been growing in Singapore. There is now much greater flexibility in our education and training system to take into account individuals' different areas of strength. Some of us are very good with numbers but not so good with words, some the other way around. A streaming system that conflates scores across different sets of ability was not the most effective way to bring out the best in our young.

The Ministry of Education has undertaken a major shift in this direction with the implementation of full subject-based banding in secondary schools. Students will have the opportunity to take subjects, at a higher or lower level, based on their strengths. It will stretch their potential in subjects they are strong in while giving them more time and space to develop in areas they need more help with. This is what broad meritocracy looks like.

Broad meritocracy must extend beyond schools to the workplace. There is little point in having a school system that recognises different areas of strength if the workplace does not reward them equitably. At the risk of sounding like a broken record, let me say this again: let us give greater recognition and reward to a broader range of skills and attributes in the jobs market.

But more important for the success of a broad meritocracy are the values that we subscribe to as a society: that every skill is recognised, every job has dignity. On that note, let me add a small point. When we speak of alternative peaks of excellence to academic excellence, we often speak of the arts, music, sports, and so on. We need to go beyond that. Talent in the arts or music is rarer than in academics; it is really a gift. The same is probably true of sports to some extent. We need to recognise excellence in more diverse fields: the warmth and care of a nurse, the empathy of a social worker, the creativity of a designer, the workmanship of a carpenter, the culinary skills of a chef, and so on.

Broadening our meritocracy should not mean a slide into mediocrity. Excellence must continue to be the hallmark of our meritocratic society. We just need to recognise and celebrate that excellence in more and more areas of work.

Second, an inclusive meritocracy. Our meritocracy has over the years become rather sharply defined, especially in our schools. There has been too much anxiety over single-digit differences in scores at the Primary School Leaving Examinations (PSLE). Making too fine a distinction in test scores is not necessarily reflective of actual differences in ability and calibre.

The Ministry of Education is moving away from fine differentiations in PSLE scoring. This will lead to more mixing across abilities and backgrounds in our schools, which is consistent with a more inclusive meritocracy. Of course, we cannot totally ignore exam scores in allocating places in secondary school. But there are benefits to having more diversity and ways could be explored to strike the right balance.

Again, an inclusive meritocracy cannot stop at our schools but must extend to the workplace. Life trajectories should not be overly determined by grades earned in schools. In many of our businesses, there is still too much emphasis on educational qualifications during recruitment and interviews, which tend to favour particular skill sets and attributes over others and may not be what the employer really wants. I have been told quite often that a six-month internship on the job tells far more about a candidate's suitability and likelihood to do well than analysing resumes and conducting interviews. Internships also give those who may have missed getting top grades the opportunity to demonstrate on the job their capabilities and strengths.

Third, a compassionate meritocracy. The role that both society and luck play in the success of individuals is often underestimated. Ben

Bernanke, former Chairman of the United States Federal Reserve System, puts it quite dramatically:

> *A meritocracy is a system in which the people who are the luckiest in their health and genetic endowment; luckiest in terms of family support, encouragement, and, probably, income; luckiest in their educational and career opportunities; and luckiest in so many other ways difficult to enumerate — these are the folks who reap the largest rewards. The only way for even a putative meritocracy to hope to pass ethical muster, to be considered fair, is if those who are the luckiest in all of those respects also have the greatest responsibility to work hard, to contribute to the betterment of the world, and to share their luck with others.*[11]

Bernanke's depiction of the centrality of luck in a meritocracy reflects the US situation more than Singapore's. Yet, there is quite some truth in what he says. Many of us in Singapore believe that the success we have achieved is through our ability and our effort, and while this is indeed true in good measure, we often forget that it also took a village and a fair amount of luck in helping us get where we are. If we take our meritocracy too literally, we could fall into the trap of an entitlement mentality: "I worked hard, I deserve what I have, and I don't owe anything to those who did not put in as much effort." Let us not forget how much help we have gotten from others; how much fortune has favoured us in our life journey. That should give us a lot more humility, to feel less entitled, more grateful and more compassionate to those less fortunate.

A Beacon for Diversity

Next, Singapore as a beacon for diversity. Many societies are struggling with diversity — differences in socio-economic status and opportunity, in values and culture, in political affiliations, in ethnicity and religion. The voices of balance and reason have become quieter; the voices of anger and resentment have become louder. The Irish poet William Butler Yeats wrote these words 100 years ago:

> *Things fall apart; the centre cannot hold; …*
> *The best lack all conviction, while the worst are full of*
> *passionate intensity.*[12]

Singapore too is seeing greater diversity across multiple fronts — nationality, ethnicity, cultural values, political views and belief systems. Diversity that is not managed well has fractured societies. Like technology, diversity is double-edged: it can be either a force for good or bad, depending on how we manage it and harness its energy.

It comes down to values rather than policies: values like keeping an open mind, developing empathy and being gracious.

First, keeping an open mind to different views. We must develop a greater commitment to evidence-based analysis and the courage to change our minds when confronted with contrary evidence. To quote George Bernard Shaw:

> *Progress is impossible without change, and those who cannot*
> *change their minds cannot change anything.*[13]

It helps if we can hold our convictions lightly, continually seek truth from facts and make an effort to look for evidence that challenges our own beliefs. It is hard to have a meaningful discussion if we are not open to the possibility of changing our views. If we are not open to changing our views, then let us at least be open to learning from other points of view. This is especially important in the world of social media, which often acts as an echo chamber of our own views.

As a society, we must master the art of respectful disagreement. We need to establish good norms, common vocabulary and trusted platforms for constructive discourse to navigate differences in views and build common ground. Understanding there are benefits and costs arising from almost any course of action sensitises us to the complexity of many issues and the need to find a middle ground. For Singapore to become a beacon for diversity, we need to develop a strong capability for healthy civic discourse, where we accept that people have different preferences and points of view but we respect one another, think through our differences and find compromises.

Second, developing empathy to understand how the other party feels. Each of us has our own story; our views, values and emotions are shaped by our life experiences. As former US President Barack Obama said in one of his speeches:

> *I think we should talk more about our empathy deficit — the ability to put ourselves in someone else's shoes; to see the world through those who are different from us — the child who's hungry, the laid-off steelworker, the immigrant woman cleaning your dorm room.*[14]

The reason behind many disagreements is that lived reality is not in accord with statistical facts. Take, for instance, the frequently expressed concerns about job security or discriminatory hiring. Yet, during the first quarter of this year, net jobs for locals increased by 24,000 and there were 68,000 vacancies remaining at the end of the quarter, with many businesses complaining they are short of staff.[15] But for those who have lost jobs, know of friends who have lost jobs or seen a less-qualified foreigner being employed in place of a local, that is their lived reality and it is at variance from the statistical facts. Although these cases do not represent the totality of the situation, they are very real for those who are adversely affected; and there were 82,000 unemployed residents at the end of the first quarter.[16] Yet, it does not change the larger reality: we are a labour-short economy facing acute skills shortages that we have had to rely on well-qualified foreigners to fill.

This is where empathy comes in. We should not reject statistical facts just because our own lived reality is at variance with them; nor should we trivialise anyone's lived reality as a mere exception to statistical facts —

because the pain for him or her is real. There is some discriminatory hiring; let us stamp it out. There have been fake certificates presented by some Employment Pass holders; let us send them back. But let us not over-generalise. Let us also acknowledge that many foreigners who come here to work are highly qualified, passionate about their work and decent people. They work hard, keep late nights, deliver good products and services, and contribute to our society.

One of my favourite poems I read as a child is titled "The Blind Men and the Elephant" by John Godfrey Saxe. It starts like this:

It was six men of Indostan, to learning much inclined, who went to see the Elephant, though all of them were blind, that each by observation might satisfy his mind.[17]

I will not read the whole poem, many of you would know how it goes: the one who touched the elephant's side thought the elephant was like a wall; the one who touched the tusk thought the elephant was like a spear; the one who touched the trunk thought the elephant was like a snake; and it goes on. The last verse of the poem is instructive:

And so these men of Indostan disputed loud and long, each in his own opinion exceeding stiff and strong, though each was partly in the right, and all were in the wrong![18]

In much of our public discourse, we are sometimes like the blind men of Indostan, holding on firmly to our own narrow perspectives and missing the larger picture. But if we could share and aggregate our limited perspectives, we can form a clearer picture and a better understanding.

Third, being gracious. Lim Siong Guan, former Head of the Civil Service and the fourth S R Nathan Fellow, spoke of a gracious society in his lecture and recounted how so many Singaporeans that he polled listed a gracious society as one of their top wishes for Singapore.[19] This augurs well for constructive, respectful debate. Unfortunately, social media has not been helpful in this regard, and has encouraged bitterness. We could do with less labelling and personal attacks. Let us not label those who are open to welcoming foreigners into Singapore as uncaring or unpatriotic. Likewise, let us not label those unhappy with the influx of foreigners as racist or xenophobic. Let us not pounce on every mistake people or the government makes; everyone slips once in a while. Let us be charitable and forgiving. Let us be temperate in our language, respectful in our disagreement, well-meaning in our criticism. Let us also take criticism in good spirit, without offence.

If Singapore can successfully harness its growing diversity as a source of creativity and vibrancy, within a culture of tolerance and respect for differences, we can stand out as a shining beacon for diversity in a fractious world.

A City of Giving

Can Singapore be a city of giving, a nation of volunteerism and philanthropy, serving our own community and Asia? Giving one's best for others, from simple acts of volunteering to being a centre for philanthropy, is yet another marker for an inspiring nation.

Singaporeans are becoming a more generous people. According to a 2016 report by the UK-based Charities Aid Foundation, Singapore is ranked 6th among 24 countries based on percentage of gross domestic product (GDP) donated by individuals to non-profit organisations.[20] That's not bad. The COVID-19 pandemic has brought out more of the volunteering spirit in many Singaporeans. In the latest financial year, the National Volunteer and Philanthropy Centre (NVPC) set a new record of S$102 million in donations to about 600 charities on Giving.sg, its one-stop platform to donate to local charities.[21] This was more than two-and-a-half times the money that was raised in the previous financial year. The number of volunteer sign ups through the platform also increased significantly, from 28,200 people in 2019 to about 32,300 in 2020.[22]

But it is the human stories of giving that are more inspiring than the numbers. There have been so many of such stories during the height of the COVID-19 pandemic last year. Two young hawkers who ran a stall at Hong

Lim Food Centre started an initiative to serve food to anyone who was unable to afford meals, no questions asked. With a touch of humour, they named this the Beng Who Cares Foundation.[23] Together with 14 of her friends, 27-year-old Nur Fatehah created SG Healthcare Heroes to gather messages of appreciation through Instagram for our healthcare workers at the frontline fighting the pandemic.[24] Two 18-year-old students started Comm.UnitySG at the very beginning of the pandemic, a ground-up youth initiative committed to serving the homeless and displaced individuals.[25] Before the government began its mask distribution exercise, 16-year-old Beatrice Wong sewed over 300 masks and distributed them to those in need.[26] Then there is the COVID-19 Migrant Support Coalition, which organised relaxation workshops, games, help desks, and so on, to help with our migrant workers' mental well-being and mindfulness during the pandemic.[27]

Each of these small acts tell a story of inspiring kindness. The initiatives may not seem much in the grand scheme of things but they are priceless for what they say about a mindset of other-centredness and the value of caring.

Can Singapore serve as a hub for philanthropic giving, both here and in the region? Singapore is one of the largest offshore wealth management centres in the world. Singapore has more than 400 single family offices.[28] Many of them are engaged in philanthropy. We can be even more purposeful as a financial centre if the wealth being managed here can be deployed to advance development, innovation, inclusion and sustainability in Asia. There is growing interest in philanthropy and environmental sustainability among the rich of Asia. We can combine charitable minds, deployable capital and our trust premium to serve as a credible and impactful base for philanthropists to do good work in the region out of Singapore. Being a philanthropy hub will encourage the development of philanthropic advisory capabilities and good jobs for Singaporeans.

We can combine innovation with inspiration by applying innovative methods to enhance philanthropy. Donors have moved away from direct giving to exploring the use of innovative structures, with the aim of delivering the greatest impact in a sustainable manner. Modern approaches to philanthropy include setting up donor-advised funds and contributing through third-party foundations. There are venture philanthropists who adopt a venture capital model, playing an active role in guiding the future of the beneficiaries, providing early-stage financing and mentoring their leaders.

Human compassion is not bound by national borders. We are inspired and proud to be Singaporeans when we see Republic of Singapore Air Force planes take off, bearing relief supplies to help countries in our region hit by natural disasters. Less than 48 hours after the 2004 Boxing Day Tsunami hit the coast of Sumatra, the Singapore Armed Forces (SAF) activated its largest humanitarian assistance and disaster relief operation. It involved the deployment of more than 1,500 SAF personnel, three supply ships, 12 helicopters, and eight transport and utility aircrafts that carried relief supplies and helped to treat more than 5,000 patients.[29] And just two months ago, Singapore sent two planeloads of oxygen cylinders to India, which was facing an acute shortage of oxygen arising from a second wave of COVID-19 infections.[30]

It's not just the government. What's more inspiring is the charitable spirit of Singaporeans. In the aftermath of the 2008 Sichuan earthquake, the Singapore Red Cross (SRC) donated S$2 million worth of medical equipment to support hospitals in the region. This made a lasting impact five years later, when another earthquake struck Sichuan in 2013, and these hospitals relied on the same donated equipment.[31] Last year, SRC reported donations amounting to more than S$6 million for COVID-19 relief operations in China, which were received from various stakeholders — the general public, corporations and the government.[32] Just this month, the SRC reported receiving over S$7.5 million in donations from members of the public and organisations for its humanitarian response at India's time of need, helping to fund ventilators, masks and other supplies for affected communities.[33]

Our millennial generation may well set new norms for giving. They already make up about one out of five Singaporeans, and will play an increasingly prominent role in society. Better educated and more exposed to the different parts of the world than earlier generations, they have a deeper insight into the struggles and suffering that exist in the world. They may well have a more expansive vision and non-material priorities in life.

More broadly, there is a growing level of social consciousness among the young. There is greater interest in issues of social development. We see more charitable donations, ethical purchasing and more socially conscious consumption; some of them are perhaps fads or fashion statements, but I also believe that some of these reflect a deeper meaning of life dimension. Volunteering and social enterprises, in particular, have been growing throughout the last decade.

The COVID-19 crisis has vividly shown just how important the value of caring is. The American Professor of Psychology Alison Gopnik makes an important point:

> Care expands an individual agent's utilities to include the utilities and goals of another.... This kind of expansion of the self serves the same overall function as the social contract: it lets a community of people do better than any individual could.[34]

Or as Lord Baden-Powell, founder of the scouting movement, said it more simply in his last message to all the scouts of the world: "The real way to get happiness is by giving happiness to other people."[35] Singaporeans can aspire to that ideal, for ourselves and for our neighbours, as a city of giving.

A Heart for the Environment

People across the world, and in Singapore, are increasingly concerned about climate change and environmental degradation. And they want to do something about it. Climate change is becoming a powerful rallying cry to inspire people to step up to a higher cause, to take collective action for the common good of our planet.

Climate change could be the burning platform to make Singaporeans an environmentally conscious people with a heart for nature. There is probably no other area in the national agenda like climate change that combines the *imperative* to manage the existential risk posed by climate change; the *opportunity* to seize the growth engine of the future, a green economy; and the *inspiration* to rally people to take actions for a larger good.

Singaporeans are indeed becoming more environmentally conscious. According to a 2020 study by the Institute of Policy Studies (IPS), 61 per cent of Singaporeans surveyed felt that protecting the environment should be prioritised even if it results in slower economic growth and some loss of jobs.[36] This is a jump from the proportion who felt this way in previous studies in 2002 and 2012. The survey also showed higher public awareness of climate change and its impact. More than nine out of 10 people support Singapore making a shift to a low carbon economy.[37]

More individuals are taking climate-friendly actions. Most of them are motivated to preserve a liveable world for future generations. Respondents believe that individuals, businesses, community groups and the government all have a part to play in tackling climate change.

There is a range of deep values that underpin people's commitment to the environment, the same values that are congruent to a cohesive society. Some see intrinsic value in nature. Some see nature as a way to connect with people to work for a larger cause. Some believe that caring for ecosystems is crucial to caring for fellow human beings, present and future. Some see caring for the environment as personal fulfilment; others as a social responsibility; yet others as a moral necessity. All of these are inspiring values; they are about something larger than ourselves.

What will take us to the next level is for groups of like-minded people to commit to collective actions to safeguard the environment. Let us not wait for the government to organise. There are so many things we can do as individuals, as groups and as companies. I have not done this myself but a good way to start would be to calculate our own carbon footprint. I understand SP Group has launched a personal carbon footprint calculator. I know from my involvement with the Emerging Stronger Taskforce

Alliance for Action on Sustainability, of discussions to explore sophisticated carbon footprint trackers that even go into the supply chains of what we consume.

There is much that we can do to minimise our negative impact on the environment. We can do an energy audit of our homes to identify ways to be more energy efficient; we can change incandescent light bulbs to light-emitting diode (LED) lights. We can stop buying bottled water and reduce single-use plastic.

We can make a conscious effort to reduce waste. We can become a zero-waste nation and a circular economy, where we use less resources and recycle resources. We have done it with water: Singapore is the first country in the world to achieve circularity in the water sector. We collect every drop of used water, treat and purify it, and turn much of it into clean water again. We can extend the circularity principle to other areas. We can reduce food waste and plastic waste. Under the Zero Waste Masterplan, by 2030, Singapore aims to reduce by 30 per cent the amount of waste per capita that we send to our landfills.[38] That can be achieved only through collective action of all Singaporeans.

We can eat lower in the food chain. Researchers at the University of Oxford have found that cutting meat and dairy products from our diet can help to reduce one's carbon footprint from food by up to 73 per cent.[39] Perhaps we could consider cutting out meat for one day a week, taking a leaf from the Meatless Mondays movement in the US. Of course, we should take care not to gorge up on meat on Tuesdays to make up for the deficit!

We can drive less and take public transport more. I must acknowledge this is something I have not been able to do myself. But this is indeed a needle-moving change that we could strive for. According to the National Climate Change Secretariat, private cars make up the largest share of emissions by the transport sector in Singapore.[40] A 2021 study of seven European cities found that individuals who switched one trip per day from driving to cycling reduced their carbon footprint by about 0.5 tonnes over a year.[41] Initiatives like Car-Free Sundays have been trialled in Singapore and give us a glimpse of what a car-lite Singapore could look like.

A Thousand Points of Light

Former US President George H. W. Bush said at his inaugural address:

> *I have spoken of a thousand points of light, of all the community organisations that are spread like stars throughout the nation, doing good.*[42]

Singapore too must have a thousand points of light. We depend too much on the government to solve our problems. Good government is Singapore's greatest strength; it is also our greatest vulnerability, for it is a single point of failure. To some extent, we do not have much latitude. For a small young country, good government is critical; we don't have the ballast that many larger countries with long histories and deep traditions have to survive bad government. But we can try to reduce the concentration risk. Moreover, with all the complexities and challenges ahead, Singapore needs a much stronger ecosystem, multiple sources of strength: a more active citizenry that self-organises, a strong business community that takes the lead in innovation and ideas to grow the economy, an energetic civil society that champions change for the betterment of the country, a vibrant academic community that provides rigorous independent analysis and insights, a high-quality media that informs and promotes public discourse based on fact and reason, a purposeful and professional philanthropic community that makes impact on the ground, and so on — making up a thousand points of light, brightening and energising our nation.

With the growing fractures in many societies, an engaged and caring citizenry is more relevant than ever. Martin Wolf of the *Financial Times* puts it very well:

> *In today's world, citizenship needs to have three aspects: loyalty to democratic political and legal institutions and the values of*

open debate and mutual tolerance that underpin them; concern
for the ability of all fellow citizens to lead a fulfilled life; and the
wish to create an economy that allows the citizens and their
institutions to flourish.[43]

We must become a democracy of deeds, not just words. We associate democracy with debates in Parliament and political rallies during elections; and today, we have a vibrant social media scene. These are no doubt important, but they are not enough. In 1971, S. Rajaratnam, one of Singapore's founding fathers, spoke of a "democracy of deeds", a democracy based on public-spirited action to solve society's problems.[44] He explains that a real democracy is "one in which the various activities in a society are distributed as widely as possible among the people."[45]

Building an innovative economy and an inclusive society is a collective national effort. The government has made major moves over the years to expand social safety nets and promote opportunities for all. Maybe it can do more, maybe it can do less. But the government alone cannot create an innovative economy or an inclusive society. That must be a collective, national endeavour. Private sector partners, employers and enterprises, the labour movement, community groups and individuals must do our part, and work closer to promote innovation and more equitable outcomes.

We need a multi-polar social compact. The social compact cannot be just between government and people; more important is the compact among the various parts of a society, an understanding on how to work together for a better society. Successful citizens should be prepared to pay the taxes necessary to sustain a society of opportunity for all. Businesses should understand they have obligations to the societies they operate in and put purpose into profit. They must help create an inclusive workforce that recognises the dignity of labour and fair wages and enable lifelong learning.

A thousand points of light will take some getting used to. The government is trying to be less directive and more collaborative; less transactional and more relational. It is progressively building up these muscles. Many parts of our society are responding constructively. But it does mean more diverse views, more public debate, more messiness and maybe even more confusion before there is consensus or compromise. We need to be able to handle this. Messiness and uncertainty are par for the course in the world of innovation; we should all get used to it. It is the sign of a maturing society and the basis for a more durable nation.

Singapore has the makings of a thousand points of light. A young former colleague of mine pointed me to American political scientist Robert Putnam's latest book *The Upswing*. According to Putnam, what fuels the upswing in a society is a widespread moral awakening — youths arise with a new set of ideals, leaders with a strong moral compass capitalise on this to push for reforms, businessmen look beyond profits to give back to their workers and communities, the ordinary citizen champions a cause larger than his own.

Then she adds, and let me quote her:

> *I do believe that there are many such Singaporeans — concerned citizens quietly seeking out ways to contribute. They are the "salt and light" — scattered everywhere, mostly invisible, yet giving the world its flavour and its form. We have to find a way to give voice to them, so that it creates a larger movement that carries all of us forward.*

These lectures are named after our former President S R Nathan. The values that guided Mr Nathan's life are an inspiration to all of us. He rose from humble beginnings to come up in life, through determination, discipline and dedication. He put country before self; he risked his own life during the Laju hijacking incident in 1974 when he secured the release of Singaporeans held hostages. He had genuine warmth and compassion for others, especially the less fortunate in society whom he went out of his way to help. Let us reflect on Mr Nathan's life of integrity and purpose in the service of others. At the end of his memoirs, a signed copy of which I treasure, he says, "Ultimately, in all the decisions I was called upon to make, my conscience was my compass."[46] Let it be so for us too, in our work and in our lives.

Change presents opportunity. This lecture series began with the changes coming through the four horsemen. Singapore is in a strong position to deal with these changes. But we need more *innovation* — because we want to find better ways of solving our problems and creating opportunity. We need more *inclusion* — because we want to benefit as many people as possible and leave no one behind. We need more *inspiration* — because amidst all the challenges around us, there is hope in a better Singapore if we stay together, and work together. Ours must not be a narrative of constraint, but a narrative of confidence; not a mindset of cynicism, but a mindset of idealism. Confidence based on strength, and idealism based on pragmatism.

Let me close with some lines from two of my favourite poets, Rabindranath Tagore and Alfred Tennyson. I don't know if they are relevant to these lectures, but like all things in literature, their meaning is what we make of them in our own minds.

The first is from Tagore's poem *Where The Mind Is Without Fear*, from his anthology *Gitanjali*, where he paints his vision for a free and cohesive India, nearly 40 years before its independence:

> *Where the world has not been broken up into fragments*
> > *by narrow domestic walls;*
> *Where words come out from the depths of truth;*
> *Where tireless striving stretches its arms towards perfection; ...*
> *Where the clear stream of reason has not lost its way*
> > *into the dreary desert sand of dead habit; ...*
> *Into that heaven of freedom, my Father, let my country awake.*[47]

The second is from Tennyson's poem *Ulysses*, and describes how, after the weary 10-year Trojan War, the Greek hero Ulysses sets sail with his men across the Mediterranean.

> *The lights begin to twinkle from the rocks:*
> *The long day wanes: the low moon climbs: the deep*
> *Moans round with many voices. Come, my friends,*
> *'Tis not too late to seek a newer world.*[48]

Notes

1. KPMG, "Report: Technology Innovation Hubs," July 16, 2021, https://www.kpmg.us/content/dam/global/pdfs/2021/tech-innovation-hubs-2021.pdf, 5.

2. Nominal wage data is from the Ministry of Manpower's Comprehensive Labour Force Surveys on the Gross Monthly Income from Work (Excluding Employer CPF) of Full-Time Employed Resident Workers. Real wage growth data are MAS staff estimates, obtained from deflating nominal wage growth by All Items CPI.

3. BBC Radio 4, "From Moral to Market Sentiments: 2020: Mark Carney — How We Get What We Value," *The Reith Lectures*, December 2, 2020, https://www.bbc.co.uk/programmes/m000py8t.

4. Barry Schwartz, "Money for Nothing," *The New York Times*, July 2, 2007, https://www.nytimes.com/2007/07/02/opinion/02schwartz.html.

5. Bruno S. Frey and Felix Oberholzer-Gee, "The Cost of Price Incentives: An Empirical Analysis of Motivation Crowding-Out," *The American Economic Review* 87, no. 4 (September 1997): 749.

6. Tharman Shanmugaratnam, "Making Ours an Uplifting Society," March 4, 2021, https://www.csc.gov.sg/articles/making-ours-an-uplifting-society.

7. Karl Marx and Frederick Engels, Address of the Central Committee to the Communist League, speech given by Karl Marx, London, March 1850.

8. Winston Churchill, "Speech to the House of Commons," November 11, 1947, *Hansard Parliamentary Debates* 444 (1947): 207.

9. Lucinda Riley, *The Seven Sisters* (London: Pan Books, 2018), 137.

10. Isaac Asimov, "What Is Intelligence Anyway?" accessed July 26, 2021, https://talentdevelop.com/articles/WIIA.html.

11. Ben S. Bernanke, "The Ten Suggestions," speech given at Baccalaureate Ceremony in Princeton University, Princeton, June 2, 2013.

12. William Butler Yeats, "The Second Coming", in *The Collected Poems of W. B. Yeats* (New York City: Collier Books, 1989), first published in *The Dial* (November 1920).

13. George Bernard Shaw, "Chapter XXXVII: Creed and Conduct," in *Everybody's Political What's What?* (New York: Dodd, Mead & Company, 1944).

14. Barack Obama, Address to Northwestern University Graduates, speech given at Northwestern University Commencement, Illinois, 2006.

15. Ministry of Manpower, *Labour Market Report First Quarter 2021* (Singapore: Ministry of Manpower, 2021), 21.
16. Ibid., A2.
17. John Godfrey Saxe, "The Blind Men and the Elephant (1872)," accessed July 20, 2021.
18. Ibid.
19. Siong Guan Lim, *Can Singapore Fall: Making the Future for Singapore* (Singapore: World Scientific, 2018), 79.
20. Charities Aid Foundation, "Gross Domestic Philanthropy: An International Analysis of GDP, Tax and Giving," January 2016, https://www.cafonline.org/docs/default-source/about-us-policy-and-campaigns/gross-domestic-philanthropy-feb-2016.pdf, 7.
21. NVPC, "NVPC Celebrates the Generosity of Singapore with New Historic Milestone Surpassing $100M in Donations," *City of Good,* April 13, 2021, https://cityofgood.sg/newsroom/nvpc-celebrates-the-generosity-of-singapore-with-new-historic-milestone-surpassing-100m-in-donations.
22. Theresa Tan, "Singaporeans Donated Record Sums Online in 2020, Despite Worst Recession Since 1965," *The Straits Times*, January 4, 2021, https://www.straitstimes.com/singapore/singaporeans-donated-record-sums-to-online-donation-portals-in-2020-despite-worst.
23. Jae Chia, "No Questions Asked: This 'Beng' Hawker Gives Away Free Meals, Has Spent Over S$15K So Far," *Vulcan Post*, 2020, https://vulcanpost.com/713051/beng-who-cares-foundation-singapore.
24. Syahindah Ishak, "S'porean Youth, 27, Starts Initiative to Honour Healthcare Workers Following Reports of Discrimination," *Mothership*, June 30, 2021, https://mothership.sg/2021/06/sg-healthcare-heroes-initiative.
25. Melissa Yip, "Students Moved to Help the Needy After Chance Encounter," *The Straits Times*, June 8, 2020, https://www.straitstimes.com/singapore/students-moved-to-help-the-needy-after-chance-encounter.
26. "Siblings Sew and Donate over 300 Masks to the Needy," *Gov.sg*, July 10, 2020, https://www.gov.sg/article/siblings-sew-and-donate-over-300-masks-to-the-needy.
27. NVPC, "A Breath of Fresh Air for Migrant Workers," *City of Good*, September 9, 2020, https://cityofgood.sg/articles/migrant-workers-rejoin-community.

28. Ministry of Trade and Industry, "Written Reply to PQ on Family Offices," Written Answer by Minister for Trade and Industry Mr Chan Chun Sing, April 5, 2021, https://www.mti.gov.sg/Newsroom/Parliamentary-Replies/2021/04/Written-reply-to-PQ-on-family-offices.

29. David Boey and Ministry of Defence, *Reaching Out: Operation Flying Eagle: SAF Humanitarian Assistance After the Tsunami* (Singapore: SNP Editions, 2005), Foreword.

30. Shabana Begum, "Singapore Sends Two Planeloads of Oxygen Cylinders to India to Aid its COVID-19 Response," *The Straits Times*, April 28, 2021, https://www.straitstimes.com/singapore/politics/singapore-sends-two-planeloads-of-oxygen-cylinders-to-india-to-aid-its-pandemic.

31. Singapore Red Cross, "Donated Hospital Equipment of 2008 Helps Survivors of Sichuan Earthquake," April 29, 2013, https://www.redcross.sg/media-centre/press-releases/272-donated-hospital-equipment-of-2008-helps-survivors-of-sichuan-earthquake.html.

32. Cindy Co, "More Than S$6 Million Raised for COVID-19 Relief: Singapore Red Cross," *CNA*, February 19, 2020, https://www.channelnewsasia.com/singapore/6-million-raised-covid19-relief-singapore-red-cross-778646.

33. Singapore Red Cross, "Singapore Red Cross Commits Further Support to Communities in Singapore and Asia Pacific Affected by COVID-19," July 6, 2021, https://redcross.sg/media-centre/press-releases/1030-singapore-red-cross-commits-further-support-to-communities-in-singapore-and-asia-pacific-affected-by-covid-19.html.

34. Alison Gopnik, "Alison Gopnik on a Revolution to Properly Value Caregivers," *The Economist*, June 18, 2021, https://www.economist.com/by-invitation/2021/06/18/alison-gopnik-on-a-revolution-to-properly-value-caregivers.

35. Robert Baden-Powell, "Baden-Powell's Last Message," *Scouts Australia*, accessed July 20, 2021, https://scouts.com.au/about/what-is-scouting/history/bps-last-message.

36. Mathew Mathews, Kay Key Teo, Melvin Tay, and Alicia Wang, "Our Singaporean Values: Key Findings from the World Values Survey," *IPS Exchange Series*, no. 16 (February 2021): 170–72.

37. National Climate Change Secretariat, "Climate Change Public Perception Survey 2019," December 16, 2019, https://www.nccs.gov.sg/media/press-release/climate-change-public-perception-survey-2019.

38. Ministry of the Environment and Water Resources, *Zero Waste Masterplan Singapore* (Singapore: Ministry of the Environment and Water Resources and National Environment Agency, 2019), 21.

39. Joseph Poore and Thomas Nemecek, "Reducing Food's Environmental Impacts through Producers and Consumers," *Science* 360, no. 6392 (2018): 991.

40. National Climate Change Secretariat, *National Climate Change Strategy 2012* (Singapore: National Climate Change Secretariat, 2012), 58.

41. Christian Brand et al., "The Climate Change Mitigation Impacts of Active Travel: Evidence from a Longitudinal Panel Study in Seven Europeans Cities," *Global Environmental Change* 67 (March 2021).

42. George H. W. Bush, "Inaugural Address of President George HW Bush," speech given at the Inauguration of the 41st President of the United States, United States Capitol, Washington, DC, January 20, 1989.

43. Martin Wolf, "Democracy Will Fall If We Don't Think As Citizens," *Financial Times*, July 6, 2020, https://www.ft.com/content/36abf9a6-b838-4ca2-ba35-2836bd0b62e2.

44. Gillian Koh, *Commentary: Volume 25: Singapore: A Democracy of Deeds and Problem-Solving* (Singapore: The National University of Singapore Society, 2016), 6.

45. Ibid., 14.

46. S R Nathan and Timothy Auger, *An Unexpected Journey: Path to the Presidency* (Singapore: Editions Didier Millet, 2011), 648.

47. Rabindranath Tagore, "Gitanjali 35," accessed July 20, 2021, https://www.poetryfoundation.org/poems/45668/gitanjali-35.

48. Alfred Tennyson, "Ulysses (1842)," accessed July 20, 2021, https://www.poetrybyheart.org.uk/poems/ulysses.

Question-and-Answer Session
Moderated by Ms Tan Su Shan

Mr Ravi Menon speaking with Ms Tan Su Shan at his Q&A session
Source: Jacky Ho for the Institute of Policy Studies

Tan Su Shan: Let me start by properly expressing the thanks of thousands of people who have read, listened or watched what you said, and ask you for your own personal take, this being the last lecture. Have you been surprised by the deluge of feedback, debate and opinions that your four lectures have sparked? I want to thank you and IPS for the huge amounts of well, you've got data, you've got poetry, a lot of new ideas, as well as a lot of heart and soul put into this, so thank you. How has the response to all your lectures been? Have you been surprised?

Ravi Menon: Su Shan, thanks for joining us. I have not been following social media responses too closely, but many people have emailed me directly, which was quite heartwarming. Some of them are people I have not met before, and they were offering ideas and support. It has been very satisfying. Some of the discussions I have seen are a bit oversimplified, but that is the nature of public discourse.

It has been quite a labour of love doing these four lectures. I now understand the meaning of the phrase — "the agony and the ecstasy", to write something from scratch when I still have a full-time day job.

Ms Tan: Running the central bank, incidentally — no small job.

Mr Menon: But the ecstasy comes from discovering new things and reflecting on issues more deeply than I would have had normally. I am happy the lectures have generated some discussion. Having respectful discussions, respectful disagreements, having empathy for another point of view — these are things I have been wanting to convey throughout my lectures. People grab ideas quickly, but behind the ideas are trade-offs, tensions and choices to be made. Almost no issue is cut and dry. If people understand the complexities, they become more open to seeing the other point of view.

Ms Tan: There are trade-offs in all choices, and ultimately, we have to make these choices, hard as they may be. Since you quoted Churchill, I thought I would also quote Churchill. I think today's inspiring nation reminds me of my own personal favourite quote of Churchill's: "You make a living by what you get, but you make a life by what you give." And I think today you were really aiming high, you were trying to lift the discourse to inspire us towards being a higher being, the epitome of Maslow's hierarchy of needs.

So let us bring this to Singapore. I think there might be some paradoxes here — we are a tiny island, we have always strived for excellence, to be the best country in the world for doing business, the most green country, the best country in managing COVID-19, and so on. This constant aim for excellence because we are small, we got to stay ahead, we got to be innovative, and so on, does that jive with this broad meritocracy that you are talking about? Because I have had a lot of questions come through and a lot of it is really about education, which I'll dive into in a minute. But also, you said you see the education broadening out. I would agree. You want to see the workplace also broaden out. I would agree. Do you see the public service also broadening out towards a more inclusive and compassionate kind of meritocracy?

Mr Menon: Yes, I think the shift towards a more inclusive meritocracy is happening in many areas. It may not be as dramatic or as fast as some would have liked because it does take time getting used to. It was easy for me to say not to just look at resumes and interviews and to broaden the way we recruit people. In practice, it is not that easy. You can understand why organisations rely a lot on exam results and interviews. People who come from a certain socio-economic class, who have travelled, who have broader exposure — they tend to do well in interviews. But interviews do not give us a really good sense of the person. I do not have an easy solution but every business needs to seriously think how it wants to recruit people.

Ms Tan: You used an analogy of a relay in your first lecture — off the gun everyone is equal, but after that when it comes to the second, third, fourth runner, it depends on how fast the guy was ahead of you. That reminds me of the first, second, third and fourth generation and how much of a head start your parents gave you or your grandparents gave your parents, and so on. So does that mean sometimes taking a step back to take two steps forward, to bring the ones behind along to this journey? And how far back do we step? I have some questions here: At what level should broad meritocracy start, given that PSLE is taken at 12 years old? Should we scrap the PSLE completely and do a different kind of testing? Is that too young? So, a few questions around how we can broaden that.

Mr Menon: There are no easy answers to this. There are a fixed number of places in the schools that are most desired, and a large number of people who want those places. When there is scarcity, how do you ration? In the marketplace, you ration by price, meaning to those who can pay for it. We definitely do not want that in our education system. The other way is to draw lots, let luck and fortune decide for us. Would that be more acceptable with people? I am not sure. Drawing lots to determine who goes where takes away the incentive and effort to want to do well. So we are still stuck with looking at some measure of achievement, be it test scores, grades, and so on.

But this is where the reforms that the Ministry of Education is making have helped: to soften and temper some of the sharp edges of meritocracy, and not to have an over-fixation with grades. I think it would be useful if we mix different abilities a little bit more; not to be too sharply defined as we are today. That means we would need to find a formula that balances between performance and more mixing. If we lean too much in the direction of mixing, then some parents will be unhappy. But if we do not blunt the influence of grades, then it is not going to be very different from today — the kids grow up with other kids who come from very similar backgrounds. We need to find a middle path. This is not purely a policy issue. I mean the policy will have to be guided by what people value, and how people feel about this. We should have a discussion. It is easy to say we should scrap something, but what would you have in its place and how will you organise things? It will be very useful if we can have that kind of discussion.

Ms Tan: There is a question from former minister, Dr Yaacob Ibrahim. He says, "Thanks Ravi for a great lecture. Just a simple question on how to realise your inspiring vision: What would be amongst the first things you would like to see happen to realise this vision?"

Mr Menon: Well, I think some of it is already happening. More consultations, more diverse views, more discussions. The government is still developing some of these muscles because we did not use them very much in the old days, but we are getting there.

Ms Tan: Also, what inspired us in the past might be different from what will inspire us in the future.

Mr Menon: That is right. There are different things that inspire people differently. So we have to start with a few different things. Philanthropy and volunteering — that is one area that some people might find inspiration in. Active citizenry is another. The environment, doing something for sustainability, that's another. Taking part in public discourses — some are inclined in that direction. Basically, we need to find more ways to bring people into civic discourse and civil society. But there will be different areas that appeal to different people.

We must do this in a way that is not overly orchestrated by the government. It needs to be truly a partnership between the public and private sectors. There are many initiatives today that bring together the private and public sectors. But the government does 70 per cent of the work, has pretty much decided what it wants, and wants some embellishments, enhancements, and a reality check from the private sector. I think that model is shifting towards one where, actually, the private sector takes the lead in shaping the outcomes and strategies, and the government sits behind and sets the broad parameters and principles that it would like to see.

Su Shan, we were just talking earlier about how we did this in the financial sector. You chaired the Private Banking Industry Group. MAS said, "Look, we need to do something about reducing the risk of money laundering and raising standards in the industry. We know the broad outcomes of what we want to achieve. But we are not private bankers, so can you all figure out how best to achieve these outcomes and develop your own standards? Your own code of conduct, your own methods to combat this risk and how you will comply with your requirements." You guys did great, and you did great as chair of the group.

Ms Tan: Thank you. I think it was a bunch of competitors in a room, thrashing out our differences, arriving at a common point of what we wanted to achieve for the industry, for Singapore. Hammering out the execution path and then off we went. And I think the results have spoken for themselves.

Mr Menon: It is good because it is industry-created. That is why it works — ground-up.

Ms Tan: So a new way to looking at this is a public–private partnership (PPP), allowing active participation from the private sector.

Mr Menon: If the government sets out clearly what the broad outcomes and broad principles are, and the OB markers if any, then we should allow the process to take shape on its own and the private sector to chart the strategies.

Ms Tan: Let us talk about the beacon of diversity. I totally empathise with putting yourself in other people's shoes. But social media is a double-edged sword. I think we are all aware that algorithms have a funny way of reinforcing your own proclivities and exacerbating this great divide between the right and left. How do we compensate for this? Can we?

Mr Menon: This is a tough problem. Many countries are facing it. I would start with finding ways to reduce the spread of falsehoods. Even before we get to the point of having people read multiple perspectives, we need to make sure that what we read, be it the single perspective in our echo chamber, is at least factually true.

Ms Tan: A fact checker of sorts.

Mr Menon: Yes. So, my vision for the Internet of the future is that there is an automatic fact-check for everything that is put there. This should be a requirement. I don't know who will set this requirement and how it will be implemented. But we need something like that.

Ms Tan: Maybe they can have a blockchain of verification.

Mr Menon: That could be quite expensive. Something simpler: I mean there are fact-checkers today, there are algorithms that do it quite well. If we can make that algorithm a permanent fixed feature on everything we read on social media, then we can separate fact from fiction and slow down the amplification of falsehoods.

The part on how we can expose people to different perspectives is more challenging, because people have a right to read what they want. I am just thinking out of the box here: say, you read a point of view on the Internet and there is a fact-check that confirms it is factual; then perhaps something else pops up to say, "there is however a different point of view you may want to read", and you could then click on the link. I am confident the techies out there will be able to write algorithms to make this happen. The question is whether that becomes an intrusion into one's reading pleasure. But today we are already being disturbed by advertisements when we read something online. You are listening to something and an advertisement pops up. Why can't something pop up that says, "There is a different point of view from what you have been just hearing"? And maybe you'll click that and listen.

Ms Tan: That might well work. It is worth trying.

Mr Menon: It is a big problem and we have to get creative about solving it.

Ms Tan: Let us now move to the city of giving. I have a question here: For many countries with active charitable non-profit sectors, compassion goes hand in hand with the desire to change. In line with our vision to become a city of giving, do you agree that increasing our openness to advocacy could help increase our inclination to give?

Mr Menon: There are already many advocacy groups in Singapore. I think in the environment space, they are quite vocal and have been able to get their point of view across. If you look back 10 or 15 years ago, it has come quite some way. Civil society is more active now and the government makes it an important priority to engage them actively.

Ms Tan: And to harness that energy that comes from advocacy for greater good.

Mr Menon: Can we do better? Of course we can. The government's muscles for engaging civil society are half developed now. With practice, it is getting better. It is also important for advocacy groups to understand that there are multiple priorities and perspectives on any given equation. Advocacy groups are built primarily around a cause that they are passionate about and such passion is important. But there are also other causes and other considerations. The education that is required is two-way — for the government to be more comfortable dealing with some of these differences and diversities, and also for these advocacy groups to understand that there are other considerations. The social compact is not just between the government and the people, but more importantly, it should become among the people. The government is just one player, a pretty important one no doubt, and an arbiter perhaps. If various groups can have respectful discussions, then we can get a better understanding and empathy for our differences.

Ms Tan: We are getting there. We have another question: With the recent show of a few examples of racism, how do you see our multiculturalism continuing to play a role to allow these thousand lights to shine?

Mr Menon: COVID-19 has brought out some of the best in us; I mentioned quite a number of examples. It has also brought out some of the worst in us — the stresses and tensions, mental fatigue have played out in this area.

On race and religion, there have always been issues. But the situation in Singapore, in perspective, is so much better than in most countries and societies we can think of. The various communities here have worked very hard at it because we know what is at stake if we get it wrong. But there will always be some who feel differently. Some of the racial incidents that have happened may not entirely be a bad thing, because I think they have brought some issues into the open — and there is greater consciousness that these are issues we need to talk about.

I think Minister Lawrence Wong's speech on the subject is probably one of the most insightful in the past several decades. It goes back to empathy again: for example, for the majority to appreciate that it is not easy to be a minority even if all the rules are fair. It is inherently more difficult to be a minority. The minorities in turn should appreciate that the majority has made substantial adjustments to accommodate multiracialism. Singapore separated and became independent over that issue — we wanted to be multiracial. Being multiracial meant the majority giving up some of what it could have had. So again it comes to empathy, understanding that the other side has given something. If all sides understand this, there is greater scope for true harmony.

Ms Tan: Both sides need to better understand and play their parts. Let us move on to the love for the environment because I feel like we should give this some time and I do not have a lot of time left. And we have talked a lot about creating a greener city. There was a question about the path of the individual versus the collective. It is quite easy for corporates, or leadership to say, look, we want to set a net zero target by 2030, 2040, 2050. But it is the getting there, the different glide paths, the individual industry best practice, the different measurements of verification, transparency, transactions. And frankly, building the capability to do so. So, what is the role of the government there? Maybe you can share a little bit in the time we have left on how you see that playing out.

Mr Menon: Net zero is going to be one of the most challenging tasks ahead. It involves major restructuring of entire economies and societies — how economies function, how business models are going to work, how societies function and how people are going to live their lives. Net zero is no easy goal, given where the world is. This is going to be big, I think the biggest change since the Industrial Revolution, maybe even bigger. The need to reduce carbon emissions has come upon us like a sudden realisation: people have been warning about this for many years, but now it has hit us in the face.

Ms Tan: Look at the flooding, the heatwaves and the suffering.

Mr Menon: We can see climate change happening and people have woken up. There is much work to be done on the sustainability journey and many capabilities that need to be built up; a lot of data that needs to be collected, a lot of technology that needs to be applied, a lot of skills that people need to have in doing this kind of work.

How are we going to make these transitions? In my second lecture, I mentioned the Ruhr industrial region in Germany and how they moved out of coal mining. It was a 20-year process, to avoid the kind of dislocations of local communities, like what happened in the Appalachians in America. The transition to sustainability takes time, effort and planning. It is going to occupy a big part of everyone's time in future — businesses, governments and people.

It is much easier to set long-term targets. There are many countries and corporations that have set a net zero target for 2050. Singapore has said as soon as possible after 2050. It is the way Singapore does things, unless we have worked out a clear strategy to get there, we would not set a definitive target. While it is impressive that so many corporations and countries have declared net zero targets, I do wonder if they have really worked out how they are going to get there.

Ms Tan: And, you know, the devil's in the details. And the scope, one, two and three emissions, how do you measure that? I think the hard work has begun. It is going to be enormous, and it is upon us and we have got to do it. I'm going to ask the last question. This is about creative destruction: Will creativity and innovation result in a less orderly society? Do you think the government is prepared for this? This creative destruction. And how prepared do you think we as individuals are for this as well?

Mr Menon: The short answer is that it varies across people and even within the government. Within the government, there are those who are prepared for a bit more fluidity and messiness and see that as part of the organic process of innovation. Others place a high premium on stability because if things go wrong, we may not be able to put it back together again. Much of the government is a microcosm of public views, and the public's own appetite for messiness varies, doesn't it?

Take Airbnb, for example. Some members of the public take the view, "Let's promote innovation and not restrict enterprise too much." Yet others say, "I do not want strangers walking through my housing complex." I am not making excuses for the government, but it is rather unfair to ask the government, "Are you prepared for messiness?" Actually the bigger question is, "Are most citizens prepared for messiness?" If we are, then let's go for it. The thing is we are not. There are parts of the public that value predictability, structure, stability, and so on. They are not wrong to value it because those attributes have gotten Singapore this far.

Ms Tan: An interesting question here about cultivating values: Whilst we have had these values demonstrated now during COVID-19, can we be more systematic in cultivating these values in our citizens rather than leaving it to chance?

It is interesting. I was just thinking about this because you are aiming high and appealing to our higher instincts. But, you know human beings, we are all born different. And sometimes, we can be a bit lazy and we might litter or speed, and take the easy way out. I like to joke that Singapore is a fine city. We get fined for doing bad things. And today's social media, in a way, plays that role to stop people from bad behaviours. Some countries have millions of cameras for surveillance to stop bad behaviours. But how do you cultivate these values more actively? Other than rely on OB markers, cameras or rules.

Mr Menon: Practice.

Ms Tan: Practice makes perfect.

Mr Menon: I think it was Aristotle who said it, more than 2,000 years ago. The way to build virtue is to practise it; that you become just by doing just acts, that you become brave by doing brave acts, that you become temperate by doing temperate acts. If pockets of people start doing that, it will get noticed, it will spread and it will become real.

Ms Tan: And I think it is true. You do derive happiness from helping other people become happier. And the notions of gratefulness and humility are important ones.

We've run out of time, but I think I speak for everyone — thank you Ravi, for the four lectures, it has been a wonderful journey that we have ridden with you. We have learnt a lot, so thank you for your gracious sharing.

Bibliography

Ang, Li Wei, Cindy Lim, Vernon Jian Ming Lee, Stefan Ma, Wei Tiong, Peng Lim Ooi, Raymond Tzer Pin Lin, Lyn James, and Jeffery Cutter. "Influenza-Associated Hospitalizations, Singapore, 2004–2008 and 2010–2012." *Emerging Infectious Diseases* 20, no. 10 (October 2014): 1652–60.

"A School for Small Families." *The Economist* 430, no. 9128 (February 2, 2019): 56–58.

Asimov, Isaac. "What Is Intelligence Anyway?" Accessed July 26, 2021. https://talentdevelop.com/articles/WIIA.html.

Australia Taxation Office. "Taxation Statistics 2018–19 Individuals: Average and Median Taxable Income, Salary or Wages, and Total Income, by Occupation and Sex." Accessed July 20, 2021. https://data.gov.au/data/dataset/taxation-statistics-2018-19/resource/47b26cb2-a680-444f-99ab-e94ed4ae9886?inner_span=True.

Baden-Powell, Robert. "Baden-Powell's Last Message." *Scouts Australia*. Accessed July 20, 2021. https://scouts.com.au/about/what-is-scouting/history/bps-last-message.

Bankmycell. "Number of Smartphones & Mobile Phone Users Worldwide." [2016–2021 data]. Accessed July 5, 2021. https://www.bankmycell.com/blog/how-many-phones-are-in-the-world.

BBC Radio 4. "From Moral to Market Sentiments: 2020: Mark Carney — How We Get What We Value." *The Reith Lectures*, December 2, 2020. https://www.bbc.co.uk/programmes/m000py8t.

Begum, Shabana. "Singapore Sends Two Planeloads of Oxygen Cylinders to India to Aid its COVID-19 Response." *The Straits Times*, April 28, 2021. https://www.straitstimes.com/singapore/politics/singapore-sends-two-planeloads-of-oxygen-cylinders-to-india-to-aid-its-pandemic.

Bernanke, Ben S. "The Ten Suggestions." Speech given at Baccalaureate Ceremony in Princeton University. Princeton, June 2, 2013.

Blanchflower, David, and Stephen Machin. "Falling Real Wages." *CentrePiece* 19, no. 1 (Spring 2014): 19–21.

Boey, David, and Ministry of Defence. *Reaching Out: Operation Flying Eagle: SAF Humanitarian Assistance After the Tsunami*. Singapore: SNP Editions, 2005.

Brainerd, Elizabeth. "Can Government Policies Reverse Undesirable Declines in Fertility?" *IZA World of Labor*, May 2014. https://wol.iza.org/uploads/ articles/23/pdfs/can-government-policies-reverse-undesirable-declines-in-fertility.pdf.

Brand, Christian, Thomas Götschi, Evi Dons, Regine Gerike, Esther Anaya-Boig, Ione Avila-Palencia, Audrey de Nazelle, Mireia Gascon, Mailin Gaupp-Berghausen, Francesco Iacorossi, Sonja Kahlmeier, Luc Int Panis, Francesca Racioppi, David Rojas-Rueda, Arnout Standaert, Erik Stigell, Simona Sulikova, Sandra Wegener, and Mark J. Nieuwenhuijsen. "The Climate Change Mitigation Impacts of Active Travel: Evidence from a Longitudinal Panel Study in Seven Europeans Cities." *Global Environmental Change* 67 (March 2021): 102–224.

Brandt, Richard. "What's Cooking Chef Watson?" *IBM*, June 6, 2017. https://www. ibm.com/blogs/think/nl-en/2017/06/06/whats-cooking-chef-watson.

Bughin, Jacques, and Susan Lund. "The Ascendancy of International Data Flows." *McKinsey Global Institute*, January 9, 2017. https://www.mckinsey.com/mgi/ overview/in-the-news/the-ascendancy-of-international-data-flows#.

Bush, George H. W. "Inaugural Address of President George HW Bush." Speech given at the Inauguration of 41st President of the United States. United States Capitol, Washington, DC, January 20, 1989.

Calvin, William H. "The Great Climate Flip-Flop." *The Atlantic* 281, no. 1 (January 1998): 47–64.

Cao, Jing, Mun Ho, and Govinda R. Timilsina. "Impacts of Carbon Pricing in Reducing the Carbon Intensity of China's GDP." *World Bank Policy Research Working Paper* 7735 (June 2016).

Carbon Pricing Leadership Coalition. "Report of the High-Level Commission on Carbon Prices." May 29, 2017. https://static1.squarespace.com/ static/54ff9c5ce4b0a53decccfb4c/t/59b7f2409f8dce5316811916/1505227332748/ CarbonPricing_FullReport.pdf.

Central Banks and Supervisors Network for Greening the Financial System (NFGS). "NGFS Climate Scenarios for Central Banks and Supervisors." June 2020. https://www.ngfs.net/sites/default/files/medias/documents/820184_ngfs_ scenarios_final_version_v6.pdf.

Charities Aid Foundation (CAF). "Gross Domestic Philanthropy: An International Analysis of GDP, Tax and Giving." January 2016. https://www.cafonline.org/docs/default-source/about-us-policy-and-campaigns/gross-domestic-philanthropy-feb-2016.pdf.

Chestney, Nina, and Jane Chung. "Temperatures to Rise 1.5 Degrees Celsius by 2030–2052 Without Rapid Steps — U.N. Report." *Reuters*, October 8, 2018. https://www.reuters.com/article/idUSL8N1WM0JJ.

Chia, Jae. "No Questions Asked: This 'Beng' Hawker Gives Away Free Meals, Has Spent Over S$15K So Far." *Vulcan Post*, 2020. https://vulcanpost.com/713051/beng-who-cares-foundation-singapore.

Cho, Renee. "Could Climate Change Shut Down the Gulf Stream?" *State of the Planet*, June 6, 2017. https://news.climate.columbia.edu/2017/06/06/could-climate-change-shut-down-the-gulf-stream.

Chow, Angela, Stefan Ma, Ai Ei Ling, and Suok Kai Chew. "Influenza-Associated Deaths in Tropical Singapore." *Emerging Infectious Diseases* 12, no. 1 (January 2006): 114–121.

Churchill, Winston. "Speech to the House of Commons." *Hansard Parliamentary Debates* 444 (November 11, 1947): 203–321.

Climate Action Tracker. "Global Temperatures: 2100 Warming Projections." [1990–2100 data]. Accessed July 5, 2021. https://climateactiontracker.org/global/temperatures.

Co, Cindy. "More Than S$6 Million Raised for COVID-19 Relief: Singapore Red Cross." *CNA*, February 19, 2020. https://www.channelnewsasia.com/singapore/6-million-raised-covid19-relief-singapore-red-cross-778646.

Cominetti, Nye. "A Record-Breaking Labour Market — But Not All Records Are Welcome." *Resolution Foundation*, February 18, 2020. https://www.resolutionfoundation.org/comment/a-record-breaking-labour-market-but-not-all-records-are-welcome.

Corak, Miles. "Income Inequality, Equality of Opportunity, and Intergenerational Mobility." *Journal of Economic Perspectives* 27, no. 3 (Summer 2013): 79–102.

"Crony Tigers, Divided Dragons," *The Economist* 405, no. 8806 (October 13, 2012): 15–18.

Cuff, Madeleine. "Report: Why the Auto, Chemical and Electricity Sectors are in Line for a Carbon Pricing Shock." *BusinessGreen*, January 22, 2018. https://www.businessgreen.com/news-analysis/3024826/report-why-the-auto-chemical-and-electricity-sectors-are-in-line-for-a-carbon-pricing-shock.

De Grauwe, Paul. *The Limits of the Market*. Translated by Anna Asbury. Oxford and New York: Oxford University Press, 2017.

DeSilver, Drew. "For Most U.S. Workers, Real Wages Have Barely Budged in Decades." *Pew Research Center*, August 7, 2018. https://www.pewresearch.org/fact-tank/2018/08/07/for-most-us-workers-real-wages-have-barely-budged-for-decades.

D'Souza, Gypsyamber, and David Dowdy. "What is Herd Immunity and How Can We Achieve It With COVID-19?" *Johns Hopkins Bloomberg School of Public Health*, April 6, 2021. https://www.jhsph.edu/COVID-19/articles/achieving-herd-immunity-with-COVID19.html.

European Commission. "Education and Training Monitor 2020: Figure 45: Adult (Aged 25–64) Participation in Learning, 4-Week Reference Period, 2010 and 2019." Accessed July 20, 2021. https://op.europa.eu/webpub/eac/education-and-training-monitor-2020/en/chapters/chapter6.html.

Feldstein, Martin. "Reducing Poverty, Not Inequality." *The Public Interest* 137 (Fall 1999): 33–41.

Frey, Bruno S., and Felix Oberholzer-Gee. "The Cost of Price Incentives: An Empirical Analysis of Motivation Crowding-Out." *American Economic Review* 87, no. 4 (September 1997): 746–55.

Galka, Max. "Watch What Has Happened to the US Middle Class Since 1970." *World Economic Forum*, April 13, 2017. https://www.weforum.org/agenda/2017/04/watch-what-has-happened-to-the-us-middle-class-since-1970.

Goldin, Claudia, and Lawrence F. Katz. "The Future of Inequality: The Other Reason Education Matters So Much." August 20, 2009. https://dash.harvard.edu/bitstream/handle/1/4341691/GoldenKatz_EdIneq.pdf?sequence=1&isAllowed=y.

Gopnik, Alison. "Alison Gopnik on a Revolution to Properly Value Caregivers." *The Economist*, June 18, 2021. https://www.economist.com/by-invitation/2021/06/18/alison-gopnik-on-a-revolution-to-properly-value-caregivers.

Gould, Elise. "State of Working America Wages 2019." *Economic Policy Institute*, February 20, 2020. https://www.epi.org/publication/swa-wages-2019.

Gould, Elise, and Hilary Wething. "U.S. Poverty Rates Higher, Safety Net Weaker Than in Peer Countries." *Economic Policy Institute*, July 24, 2012. https://www. epi.org/publication/ib339-us-poverty-higher-safety-net-weaker.

Greenwood, Jeremy, Nezih Guner, Georgi Kocharkov, and Cezar Santos. "Marry Your Like: Assortative Mating and Income Inequality." *American Economic Review* 104, no. 5 (May 2014): 348–53.

Han, Jeehoon, Bruce D. Meyer, and James X. Sullivan. "Real-time Poverty Estimates during the COVID-19 Pandemic through March 2021." April 14, 2021. https://harris.uchicago.edu/files/monthly_poverty_rates_updated_thru_mar_2021. pdf.

Holder, Michael. "'Unusually Positive News': Does 2020 Mark a Turning Point for Delivering on the Paris Agreement Goals?" *BusinessGreen*, December 2, 2020. https://www.businessgreen.com/analysis/4024335/unusually-positive-news-2020-mark-point-delivering-paris-agreement-goals.

Humanitarian Organisation for Migration Economics (HOME). "Coming Clean: A Study on the Wellbeing of Bangladeshi Conservancy Workers in Singapore." August 2020. https://drive.google.com/file/d/1EqG-aQJjI29 sw7cNKRB7M64N-sJh-M4z/view.

International Energy Agency. "Net Zero by 2050: A Roadmap for the Global Energy Sector." May 2021. https://www.iea.org/reports/net-zero-by-2050.

International Labour Organization (ILO). *World Employment and Social Outlook 2018: Greening With Jobs*. Geneva: International Labour Office, 2018.

International Monetary Fund (IMF). *Fiscal Monitor: How to Mitigate Climate Change*. Washington, DC: International Monetary Fund, 2009.

International Renewable Energy Agency. "Renewable Capacity Statistics 2021." March 2021. https://www.irena.org/publications/2021/March/Renewable-Capacity-Statistics-2021.

Ishak, Syahindah. "S'porean Youth, 27, Starts Initiative to Honour Healthcare Workers Following Reports of Discrimination." *Mothership*, June 30, 2021. https://mothership.sg/2021/06/sg-healthcare-heroes-initiative.

Kim, Meeri. "The Link between Children's Academic Achievement and Family Income." *Blog on Learning & Development*, April 13, 2018. https://bold.expert/the-link-between-childrens-academic-achievement-and-family-income.

Kleeman, Alexandra. "Cooking with Chef Watson, I.B.M.'s Artificial-Intelligence App." *The New Yorker*, November 20, 2016. https://www.newyorker.com/magazine/2016/11/28/cooking-with-chef-watson-ibms-artificial-intelligence-app.

Koh, Gillian. *Commentary: Volume 25: Singapore: A Democracy of Deeds and Problem-Solving.* Singapore: The National University of Singapore Society, 2016.

KPMG. "Report: Technology Innovation Hubs." July 16, 2021. https://www.kpmg.us/content/dam/global/pdfs/2021/tech-innovation-hubs-2021.pdf.

Lazer, Leah. "How Can We Ensure a Just Transition to the Green Economy?" *World Economic Forum*, April 14, 2021. https://www.weforum.org/agenda/2021/04/how-can-we-ensure-a-just-transition-to-the-green-economy.

Lien Foundation. "Long Term Care Manpower Study." July 2018. http://www.lienfoundation.org/sites/default/files/Long%20Term%20Care%20Manpower%20Study%20FINAL_0.pdf.

Lim, Janice, and Jun Yuan Yong. "The Big Read: Undervalued and Underpaid, Singapore's Essential Services Workers Deserve Better." *Today*, June 13, 2020. https://www.todayonline.com/big-read/big-read-singapores-under-valued-essential-services-workers-how-pay-them-what-they-deserve.

Lim, Siong Guan. *Can Singapore Fall: Making the Future for Singapore.* Singapore: World Scientific, 2018.

Lindsey, Rebecca. "Climate Change: Global Sea Level." *NOAA Climate.gov,* January 25, 2021. https://www.climate.gov/news-features/understanding-climate/climate-change-global-sea-level.

Loria, Kevin. "CO2 Levels Are at Their Highest in 800,000 Years." *World Economic Forum*, May 9, 2018. https://www.weforum.org/agenda/2018/05/earth-just-hit-a-terrifying-milestone-for-the-first-time-in-more-than-800-000-years.

Manning, Alan. "The Elusive Employment Effect of the Minimum Wage." *Centre for Economic Performance Discussion Paper*, no. 1428 (May 2016).

Marx, Karl, and Frederick Engels. Address of the Central Committee to the Communist League. Speech given by Karl Marx, London, March 1850.

Mathews, Mathew, Kay Key Teo, Melvin Tay, and Alicia Wang. "Our Singaporean Values: Key Findings from the World Values Survey." *IPS Exchange Series*, no. 16 (February 2021).

Metcalf, Gilbert E., and James Stock. "Measuring the Macroeconomic Impact of Carbon Taxes." *AEA Papers and Proceedings* 110 (May 2020): 101–06.

Met Office, United Kingdom. "Global Climate in Context as the World Approaches 1°C above Pre-Industrial for the First Time." November 2015. https://www.metoffice.gov.uk/research/news/2015/global-average-temperature-2015.

Ministry of the Environment and Water Resources. *Zero Waste Masterplan Singapore*. Singapore: Ministry of the Environment and Water Resources and National Environment Agency, 2019.

Ministry of Finance, Singapore. "(2015) Income Growth, Inequality and Mobility Trends in Singapore." August 2015. https://www.mof.gov.sg/docs/default-source/default-document-library/news-andpublications/featured-reports/income-growth-distribution-and-mobility-trends-in-singapore.pdf.

Ministry of Finance, Sweden. "Sweden's Carbon Tax." Accessed July 12, 2021. https://www.government.se/government-policy/taxes-and-tariffs/swedens-carbon-tax.

Ministry of Foreign Affairs. "PM Lee on the COVID-19 Situation in Singapore." April 21, 2020. https://www.mfa.gov.sg/Overseas-Mission/Washington/Mission-Updates/2020/04/PM-Lee-on-the-COVID-19-Situation-in-Singapore-on-21-April-2020.

Ministry of Health. "Elderly with Mobility Issues." July 5, 2021. https://www.moh.gov.sg/news-highlights/details/elderly-with-mobility-issues#:~:text=With%20an%20ageing%20population%2C%20we,50%2C000%20between%202000%20and%202020.

Ministry of Manpower. "Eligibility for S Pass." Accessed July 20, 2021. https://www.mom.gov.sg/passes-and-permits/s-pass/eligibility.

———. "Factsheet — Workfare Income Supplement." https://www.mom.gov.sg/-/media/mom/documents/speeches/2010/factsheet---wis-(110310).pdf.

———. "Foreign Workforce Numbers." [2020 data]. Accessed July 20, 2021. https://www.mom.gov.sg/documents-and-publications/foreign-workforce-numbers.

———. *Labour Market Report First Quarter 2021*. Singapore: Ministry of Manpower, 2021.

———. "Median Gross Monthly Income from Work (Including Employer CPF) of Full-Time Employed Residents Aged Fifteen Years and Over by Occupation and Age." June 2020. https://stats.mom.gov.sg/Pages/Gross-Monthly-Income-Tables2020.aspx.

———. "Occupational Wages 2020." Accessed July 20, 2021. https://stats.mom.gov.
sg/Pages/Occupational-Wages-Tables2020.aspx.

———. "Report: Labour Force in Singapore: 2020 Edition." January 28, 2021. https://
stats.mom.gov.sg/iMAS_PdfLibrary/mrsd_2020LabourfForce.pdf.

———. "Services Sector: Work Permit Requirements." Accessed July 20, 2021. https://
www.mom.gov.sg/passes-and-permits/work-permit-for-foreign-worker/
sector-specific-rules/services-sector-requirements.

———. "Speech by Minister for Manpower, Mrs Josephine Teo at Debate on
President's Address." September 1, 2020. https://www.mom.gov.sg/newsroom/
speeches/2020/0901-speech-by-minister-for-manpower-mrs-josephine-teo-
at-the-debate-on-president-address.

———. "What is the Local Qualifying Salary (LQS)?" Accessed July 20, 2021. https://
www.mom.gov.sg/faq/work-pass-general/what-is-the-local-qualifying-salary.

Ministry of Trade and Industry. "The Impact of the Workfare Income Supplement Scheme
on Individuals' Labour Outcomes." August 12, 2014. https://www.mti.gov.sg/-/
media/MTI/Legislation/Public-Consultations/2014/The-Impact-Of-The-Workfare-
Income-Supplement-Scheme-on-Individuals-Labour-Outcomes/fa_2q14.pdf.

———. "Written Reply to PQ on Family Offices." Written Answer by Minister for Trade
and Industry Mr Chan Chun Sing. April 5, 2021. https://www.mti.gov.sg/Newsroom/
Parliamentary-Replies/2021/04/Written-reply-to-PQ-on-family-offices.

Mishel, Lawrence, and Jori Kandra. "Wages for the Top 1% Skyrocketed 160% since
1979 while the Share of Wages for the Bottom 90% Shrunk." *Economic Policy
Institute,* December 1, 2020. https://www.epi.org/blog/wages-for-the-top-1-
skyrocketed-160-since-1979-while-the-share-of-wages-for-the-bottom-90-
shrunk-time-to-remake-wage-pattern-with-economic-policies-that-generate-
robust-wage-growth-for-vast-majority.

Monetary Authority of Singapore (MAS). "Remarks by Mr Ravi Menon, Managing
Director, MAS, at the MAS Annual Report 2019/2020 Virtual Media Conference."
July 16, 2020. https://www.mas.gov.sg/news/speeches/2020/remarks-by-mr-
ravi-menon-at-the-mas-annual-report-2019-2020-media-conference#5.

———. "Sustainability Report 2020/2021: Managing Director's Foreword." June 9,
2021. https://www.mas.gov.sg/publications/sustainability-report/2021/
sustainability-report/foreword.

Nathan, S. R., and Timothy Auger. *An Unexpected Journey: Path to the Presidency.* Singapore: Editions Didier Millet, 2011.

National Climate Change Secretariat (NCCS). "Climate Change Public Perception Survey 2019." December 16, 2019. https://www.nccs.gov.sg/media/press-release/climate-change-public-perception-survey-2019.

———. *National Climate Change Strategy 2012.* Singapore: National Climate Change Secretariat, 2012.

———. "Singapore's Climate Action Plan: Take Action Today, For a Carbon-Efficient Singapore." 2016. https://www.nccs.gov.sg/docs/default-source/publications/take-action-today-for-a-carbon-efficient-singapore.pdf.

National Population and Talent Division, Singapore Department of Statistics, Ministry of Home Affairs, Immigration & Checkpoints Authority, and Ministry of Manpower. "Population in Brief 2020." September 2020. https://www.strategygroup.gov.sg/files/media-centre/publications/population-in-brief-2020.pdf.

National Volunteer and Philanthropy Centre (NVPC). "A Breath of Fresh Air for Migrant Workers." *City of Good*, September 9, 2020. https://cityofgood.sg/articles/migrant-workers-rejoin-community.

———. "NVPC Celebrates the Generosity of Singapore with New Historic Milestone Surpassing $100M in Donations." *City of Good,* April 13, 2021. https://cityofgood.sg/newsroom/nvpc-celebrates-the-generosity-of-singapore-with-new-historic-milestone-surpassing-100m-in-donations.

Ng, Irene Y. H., Yiying Ng, and Po Choo Lee. "Singapore's Restructuring of Low-Wage Work: Have Cleaning Job Conditions Improved?" *The Economic and Labour Relations Review* 29, no. 3 (2018): 308–27.

Ng, Tze Pin, Keng-Hock Pwee, Mathew Niti, and Lee Gan Goh. "Influenza in Singapore: Assessing the Burden of Illness in the Community." *Annals of the Academy of Medicine, Singapore* 31, no. 2 (March 2002): 182–88.

NTUC Training and Transformation. "NTUC Facilitates Cross-Sector Collaboration to Uplift, Transform and Grow the Plumbing Industry in the Next 10 Years." Accessed July 20, 2021. https://trainandtransform.ntuc.org.sg/trainandtransform/Pages/Details.aspx?ItemId=32.

Nunn, Ryan, and Jay Shambaugh. "Whose Wages Are Rising and Why?" *Policy 2020 Brookings*, January 21, 2020. https://www.brookings.edu/policy2020/votervital/whose-wages-are-rising-and-why.

Obama, Barack. Address to Northwestern University Graduates. Speech given at Northwestern University Commencement, Illinois, 2006.

OECD Centre on Well-being, Inclusion, Sustainability and Equal Opportunity (WISE). "Inequalities in Household Wealth and Financial Insecurity of Households." July 2021. https://www.oecd.org/wise/Inequalities-in-Household-Wealth-and-Financial-Insecurity-of-Households-Policy-Brief-July-2021.pdf.

Office for National Statistics, United Kingdom. "Earning and Hours Worked, Industry by Four-Digit SIC: ASHE Table 16." Accessed July 20, 2021. https://www.ons.gov.uk/employmentandlabourmarket/peopleinwork/earningsandworkinghours/datasets/industry4digitsic2007ashetable16.

Organisation for Economic Co-operation and Development (OECD). "Gini: Disposable Income, Post Taxes and Transfers." [2004–2020 data]. Accessed July 20, 2021. https://stats.oecd.org/Index.aspx?DataSetCode=IDD.

———. "P50/P10 Disposable Income Decile Ratio." [2004–2020 data]. Accessed July 20, 2021. https://stats.oecd.org/Index.aspx?DataSetCode=IDD.

———. "Issue Paper: The Distributional Aspects of Environmental Quality and Environmental Policies: Opportunities for Individuals and Households." November 2018. https://www.oecd.org/greengrowth/GGSD_2018_Households_WEB.pdf.

———. *The OECD Tax-Benefit Model for Canada: Description of Policy Rules for 2019.* Paris: OECD Publishing, 2020.

———. *The OECD Tax-Benefit Model for Poland: Description of Policy Rules for 2020.* Paris: OECD Publishing, 2020.

———. "The Role and Design of Net Wealth Taxes in the OECD." *OECD Tax Policy Studies*, no. 26 (2018).

OXFAM International. "5 Natural Disasters that Beg for Climate Action." Accessed July 5, 2021. https://www.oxfam.org/en/5-natural-disasters-beg-climate-action.

Parry, Ian, Simon Black, and James Roaf. "Proposal for an International Carbon Price Floor Among Large Emitters." *International Monetary Fund*, June 2021. https://www.imf.org/en/Publications/staff-climate-notes/Issues/2021/06/15/Proposal-for-an-International-Carbon-Price-Floor-Among-Large-Emitters-460468.

Phillips, Nicky. "The Coronavirus Is Here to Stay — Here's What That Means." *Nature* 590, no. 7846 (February 18, 2021): 382–84.

Piketty, Thomas. *Capital in the Twenty-First Century*. Translated by Arthur Goldhammer. Massachusetts: Harvard University Press, 2014.

Poore, Joseph, and Thomas Nemecek. "Reducing Food's Environmental Impacts through Producers and Consumers." *Science* 360, no. 6392 (2018): 987–92.

Pradhan, Elina. "Female Education and Childbearing: A Closer Look at the Data." *World Bank Blogs*, November 24, 2015. https://blogs.worldbank.org/health/female-education-and-childbearing-closer-look-data.

REACH. "Media Release: Majority of Singaporeans Do Not Feel Strongly Negative About Foreigners in Singapore." October 10, 2020. https://www.sgpc.gov.sg/sgpcmedia/media_releases/reach/press_release/P-20201010-1/attachment/MAJORITY%20OF%20SINGAPOREANS%20DO%20NOT%20FEEL%20STRONGLY%20NEGATIVE%20ABOUT%20FOREIGNERS%20IN%20SINGAPORE.pdf.

Riley, Lucinda. *The Seven Sisters*. London: Pan Books, 2018.

Rowling, Megan. "'Net-Zero' Emissions: What Is It and Why Does It Matter So Much?" *World Economic Forum*, September 23, 2020. https://www.weforum.org/agenda/2020/09/carbon-emissions-net-zero-global-warming-climate-change.

Sandbu, Martin. *The Economics of Belonging*. New Jersey: Princeton University Press, 2020.

———. "The Everyone Economy: How to Make Capitalism Work for All." *Financial Times*, July 3, 2020. https://www.ft.com/content/a22d4215-0619-4ad2-9054-3a0765f64620.

Saxe, John Godfrey. "The Blind Men and the Elephant (1872)." Accessed July 20, 2021.

Schwartz, Barry. "Money for Nothing." *The New York Times*, July 2, 2007. https://www.nytimes.com/2007/07/02/opinion/02schwartz.html.

Shanmugaratnam, Tharman. Speech given to the Twelfth Parliament at the Debate on Annual Budget Statement, March 5, 2014, *Hansard Parliamentary Debates* 91 (2014).

———. "Making Ours an Uplifting Society." March 4, 2021. https://www.csc.gov.sg/articles/making-ours-an-uplifting-society.

Shaw, George Bernard. "Chapter XXXVII: Creed and Conduct." In *Everybody's Political What's What?* New York: Dodd, Mead & Company, 1944.

"Siblings Sew and Donate over 300 Masks to the Needy." *Gov.sg*, July 10, 2020. https://www.gov.sg/article/siblings-sew-and-donate-over-300-masks-to-the-needy.

Shorrocks, Anthony, James Davies, Rodrigo Lluberas, and Credit Suisse Research Institute. "Global Wealth Distribution." In *Global Wealth Report 2021*, June 2021. http://docs.dpaq.de/17706-global-wealth-report-2021-en.pdf, 17–25.

Singapore Department of Statistics. "Average Monthly Household Income from Work Per Household Member (Excluding Employer CPF Contributions) Among Resident Employed Households by Deciles." [2000–2020 data]. Accessed July 20, 2021. https://tablebuilder.singstat.gov.sg/table/CT/17251.

———. "Gini Coefficient Among Resident Employed Households (Excluding Employer CPF Contributions)." [2000–2020 data]. Accessed July 20, 2021. https://tablebuilder.singstat.gov.sg/table/CT/17206.

———. "Gini Coefficient Among Resident Employed Households (Including Employer CPF Contributions)." [2020 data]. Accessed July 20, 2021. https://tablebuilder.singstat.gov.sg/table/CT/17242.

———. "Proportion of Elderly Residents (65 Years & Over) Among Resident Population." [1970–2020 data]. Accessed July 5, 2021. https://www.tablebuilder.singstat.gov.sg/publicfacing/createDataTable.action?refId=14914.

———. "Resident Labour Force." [2010–2020 data]. Accessed July 12, 2021. https://stats.mom.gov.sg/Pages/Labour-Force-Summary-Table.aspx.

———. "Singapore Supply, Use and Input-Output Tables." [2010 and 2017 data]. Accessed July 12, 2021. https://www.singstat.gov.sg/find-data/search-by-theme/economy/national-accounts/latest-data#SU-IOT.

Singapore Red Cross. "Donated Hospital Equipment of 2008 Helps Survivors Of Sichuan Earthquake." April 29, 2013. https://www.redcross.sg/media-centre/press-releases/272-donated-hospital-equipment-of-2008-helps-survivors-of-sichuan-earthquake.html.

———. "Singapore Red Cross Commits Further Support to Communities in Singapore and Asia Pacific Affected by COVID-19." July 6, 2021. https://redcross.sg/media-centre/press-releases/1030-singapore-red-cross-commits-further-support-to-communities-in-singapore-and-asia-pacific-affected-by-covid-19.html.

Swedish Environmental Protection Agency. "Territorial Emissions and Uptake of Greenhouse Gases." Accessed July 12, 2021. https://www.naturvardsverket.se/klimatutslapp.

Tagore, Rabindranath. "Gitanjali 35." Accessed July 20, 2021. https://www.poetryfoundation.org/poems/45668/gitanjali-35.

Tan, Theresa. "Singaporeans Donated Record Sums Online in 2020, Despite Worst Recession Since 1965." *The Straits Times*, January 4, 2021. https://www.straitstimes.com/singapore/singaporeans-donated-record-sums-to-online-donation-portals-in-2020-despite-worst.

Tennyson, Alfred. "Ulysses (1842)." Accessed July 20, 2021. https://www.poetrybyheart.org.uk/poems/ulysses.

Tollefson, Jeff. "How Hot Will Earth Get By 2100?" *Nature* 580, no. 7804 (April 23 2020): 444–46.

Turner, Adair. "Wealth, Debt, Inequality and Low Interest Rates: Four Big Trends and Some Implications." *Cass Business School*, March 26, 2014. https://www.cass.city.ac.uk/__data/assets/pdf_file/0014/216311/RedingNotes_Lord-Turner-Annual-Address-at-Cass-Business-School-March-26-2014.pdf.

United Nations. "LIVE: Climate Ambition Summit." *UN News*, December 12, 2020. https://news.un.org/en/story/2020/12/1079862.

United Nations Department of Economic and Social Affairs (DESA), Population Division. *World Population Ageing 2019: Highlights.* New York: United Nations, 2019.

———. "World Population Prospects 2019: Probabilistic Projections for Total Population." Accessed July 5, 2021. https://population.un.org/wpp/Graphs/Probabilistic/POP/TOT/900.

United Nations Environment Programme (UNEP). *Towards A Green Economy: Pathways to Sustainable Development and Poverty Eradication.* Paris: United Nations Environment Programme, 2011.

United States National Intelligence Council. "Global Trends 2040." March 2021. https://www.dni.gov/files/ODNI/documents/assessments/GlobalTrends_2040.pdf.

U.S. Bureau of Labor Statistics. "May 2020 National Occupational Employment and Wage Estimates United States." Accessed July 20, 2021. https://www.bls.gov/oes/current/oes_nat.htm.

U.S. Energy Information Administration. "U.S. Energy Information Administration's International Energy Outlook 2020 (IEO2020)." October 14, 2020. https://www.eia.gov/outlooks/ieo/pdf/ieo2020.pdf.

Weixel, Nathaniel. "Fauci: Herd Immunity Could Require 90 Percent of Country to be Vaccinated." *The Hill*, December 24, 2020. https://thehill.com/policy/healthcare/531611-fauci-herd-immunity-could-require-90-percent-of-country-to-be-vaccinated.

Wolf, Martin. "Democracy Will Fall If We Don't Think as Citizens." *Financial Times*, July 6, 2020. https://www.ft.com/content/36abf9a6-b838-4ca2-ba35-2836bd0b62e2.

Woloszko, Nicolas, and Orsetta Causa. "Housing and Wealth Inequality: A Story of Policy Trade-Offs." *VoxEU*, March 31, 2020. https://voxeu.org/article/housing-and-wealth-inequality-story-policy-trade-offs.

Workfare, Singapore. "Factsheet on Enhancements to the Workfare Income Supplement Scheme." February 2019. https://www.workfare.gov.sg/Press%20Releases/Pages/PressRelease_Feb2019.pdf.

World Bank. "Carbon Pricing Dashboard: Map & Data." [2021 data]. Accessed July 5, 2021. https://carbonpricingdashboard.worldbank.org/map_data.

World Bank Group. *States and Trends of Carbon Pricing 2019*. Washington, DC: The World Bank, 2019.

World Economic Forum (WEF). *The Global Competitiveness Report 2019*. Geneva: World Economic Forum, 2019.

World Health Organization (WHO). "Up to 650 000 People Die of Respiratory Diseases Linked to Seasonal Flu Each Year." December 13, 2017. https://www.who.int/news/item/13-12-2017-up-to-650-000-people-die-of-respiratory-diseases-linked-to-seasonal-flu-each-year.

Yeats, William Butler. "The Second Coming." In *The Collected Poems of W. B. Yeats*, 186–187. New York City: Collier Books, 1989. First published in *The Dial*, November 1920.

Yip, Melissa. "Students Moved to Help the Needy After Chance Encounter." *The Straits Times*, June 8, 2020. https://www.straitstimes.com/singapore/students-moved-to-help-the-needy-after-chance-encounter.

Zetter, Kim. "Senate Panel: 80 Percent of Cyber Attacks Preventable." *Wired*, November 17, 2009. https://www.wired.com/2009/11/cyber-attacks-preventable.

Index

www.ingramcontent.com/pod-product-compliance
Lightning Source LLC
Chambersburg PA
CBHW061248220326
41599CB00028B/5574